MW01002321

Additional Praise for *INSPIRED*

"Dean's adventures prove that the more you give to the areas you visit, the more you receive in return."

—Peter Hillary

"Dean reminds us that to go into the wilderness is to experience magic, power, and beauty, but also mystery. Without mystery there is no adventure. Dean's writing takes you as close as you can get on these adventures without actually going. I couldn't wait to unveil the mystery of each new page. What is even more special is what Dean is doing: Making it possible for people to push beyond their personal limits, to find courage they did not know they had, and to embrace unforgettable experiences in the wild that few people will have. But there is much more—read this book and you will want to shake his hand. Thanks, Dean, for confirming that we should not ration passion, and that the time is now."

—*National Geographic* Explorer Mike Libecki

"Dean has captured the essence and attraction of global adventures, which unite all of us who have spent our lives exploring the far reaches of our amazing planet, Mother Earth. He who does not know the world does not know his place in it; so be dauntless and daring, remembering that to participate is to live, [and that] spectators only exist."

—Dick Bass, First person to climb the Seven Summits, Developer, Snowbird Ski and Summer Resort

"Dean Cardinale is one of my favorite people to spend time with, in or out of the mountains. Dean is a true adventurer with an exceptional head and heart. In this wonderful collection Dean shares the joys and terrors of a life well spent in the mountains. He brings to life what it feels like to crawl down near the summit of Denali in a whiteout blizzard; to endure and push to the summit of Mt. Everest during a season of terrible weather; to be arrested and have your team locked in a boxcar for a week in New Guinea; and to compassionately guide a couple in their mid seventies to the top of Mt. Kilimanjaro. Besides bringing you along on his gripping journeys, Dean shares the life lessons he's learned from each adventure. This is a book you will love spending time with!"

—Geoff Tabin, M.D., Director, Himalayan Cataract Project,
Fourth person to climb the Seven Summits

"Dean combines a compassionate heart with an adventurous 'let's go' spirit. When he sees a need in the world, he takes action to correct it. Philanthropy and the world benefit."

—Frank Shankwitz, founder of the Make a Wish Foundation

"Dean Cardinale is not just a man who lives his dreams but also one who has found a way to share adventure with others and give back. Dean shows through his amazing stories that any obstacle in life can be overcome with passion, hard work and a humble attitude. From losing everything to climbing Mount Everest, Dean demonstrates what it takes to go out of your comfort zone and manifest your destiny."

—Joby Ogwyn, two time Everest summiteer and only person
in the world to fly next to Mt Everest in a wingsuit

INSPIRED

Lessons Learned From a Life of Adventure

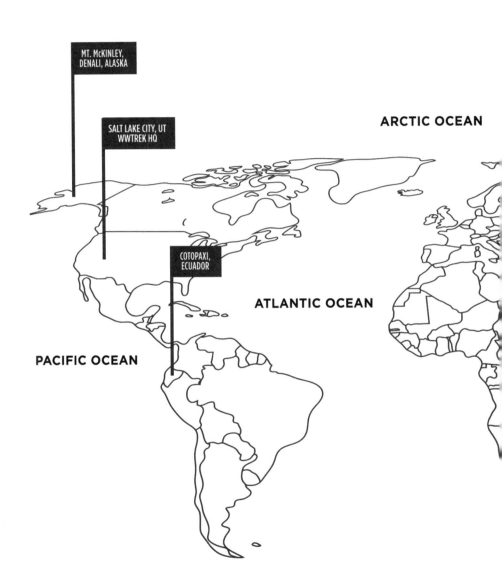

ARCTIC OCEAN

MT. McKINLEY,
DENALI, ALASKA

SALT LAKE CITY, UT
WWTREK HQ

COTOPAXI,
ECUADOR

ATLANTIC OCEAN

PACIFIC OCEAN

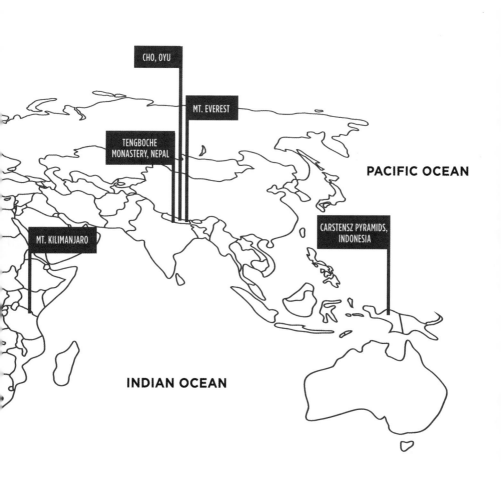

CHO, OYU

MT. EVEREST

TENGBOCHE
MONASTERY, NEPAL

PACIFIC OCEAN

CARSTENSZ PYRAMIDS,
INDONESIA

MT. KILIMANJARO

INDIAN OCEAN

A few years ago I was guiding a group to Mount Everest Base Camp in Nepal. We were in a monastery receiving a special blessing from a lama to bless us for a safe journey, [and] the lama told us, "We all cast a shadow in our lives; this is our life shadow. We can choose to cast a good shadow or a bad shadow; it is our choice." Then he looked at us and said, "Cast a good shadow."

—Lama Geshi Tengboche Monastery, Nepal

INSPIRED
Lessons Learned From a Life of Adventure
DEAN CARDINALE

For more information contact:
Dean Cardinale
www.wwtrek.com
www.humanoutreachproject.org
Phone: 801.943.0264
email: info@wwtrek.com

Hardcover ISBN: 978-0-692-43653-0
eBook ISBN: 978-0-692-43652-3

Library of Congress Control Number: 2015943410

Printed in China

CONTENTS

FOREWORD

by Geoff Tabin, M.D.

Dean Cardinale is one of my favorite people to spend time with, in or out of the mountains. His infectious enthusiasm and enjoyment of all aspects of life are contagious. Dean and I have spent time together in Nepal and Africa, and we have shared a rope on classic Wasatch rock climbs in Utah. I have also had the good fortune to see Dean in action during early powder mornings at Snowbird. One of the best phone calls anyone can receive is Dean Cardinale saying, "We are getting another foot tonight. They are closing the road at six. Meet me at the first tram!"

For his "day job," Dean works as an avalanche forecaster for the ski patrol at the Snowbird ski resort in Utah, home of "the greatest snow on earth." Prior to his current position, Dean spent several seasons as the director of the Snowbird ski patrol. Waiting in the dark for the first tram, Dean is in his element. He is mentally going over everything that needs to be done to safely open a major ski resort, calculating avalanche risk, deciding which slopes to bomb and which to open to the public. He is also working with his team and getting everyone fired up for the day. At the top of the tram, his crowd gathers in the ski patrol hut to drink strong coffee and listen as Dean maps out the plan. It is Dean's meticulous attention to detail and his understanding of the mountain, snow chemistry, and avalanche science that will allow the resort to open. At first light his crew head into the crisp mountain air, clip into their skis, and head out to do their avalanche control work. Like most of his team, Dean has a maniacal glint of excitement in his eyes.

It is powder time! After ski cutting and bombing the most dangerous slopes, Dean and company get first tracks on all the best lines. Despite having skied thousands of perfect powder pitches, Dean still loves to ski. He loves to see his friends smile, and for them to share his magical mornings. This joy, and this intense determination to live life to its fullest, are what Dean shares in this wonderful book. He also conveys the human aspect of a life of adventure. When I was conducting a cataract intervention in a remote area of Tanzania, I hired Dean to handle our logistics. Not only did he arrange transportation and support for the doctors, patients, and our equipment; he also pitched in and helped move patients, clean their faces, and instill eye-drops. We then visited the orphanage Dean built, which provides shelter for some of the poorest children on our planet. To cap that journey, Dean guided my entire family to the top of Mt. Kilimanjaro.

Dean is a true adventurer with an exceptional head and heart. In this wonderful collection he shares the joys and terrors of a life well spent in the mountains. He lets you experience vicariously what it feels like to crawl down from the summit of Denali in a whiteout blizzard, to endure and push to the summit of Mt. Everest during a season of terrible weather, to be arrested and have your team held at gunpoint and locked in a boxcar for more than a week in New Guinea, and to compassionately guide a couple in their mid seventies to the top of Mt. Kilimanjaro. Dean brings you along on these gripping journeys and shares the life lessons he has learned from each adventure. This is a book you will treasure.

AN INVITATION TO MY READERS

by Dean Cardinale

inspired (in-spīrd') adjective
Of extraordinary quality, as if arising from some external creative impulse.

This book is a direct extension of the storytelling I do while out guiding or trekking with others. I have always been a dreamer and a storyteller. It is one of the primary things I love about guiding work. You get to meet all kinds of interesting people from many walks of life and go on adventures with them. You get to hear their stories. You get to tell them yours. You have adventures together, all the while creating new stories as you go. In this way, you learn from each other. Stories teach us about the world. They impart lessons.

Stories are important precisely because they teach us things. I tell stories just for the fun of it when I am guiding people on treks and climbs around the globe, but the real purpose—or at least the greatest value—of storytelling is that it broadens your horizons, shares wisdom, and offers different perspectives.

My goal as both a guide and a storyteller is simple: I want to push people to move outside the confines of their own comfort zones. I hope that my personal stories, only a few of which have been selected and curated for this book, push people to go out and find their own adventures and learn their own lessons. I want to push people out of their comfort zones, where they will find new adventures, and hopefully, more satisfaction in life.

People often want to cling to their comfort zones. In our modern world, the successful life is sometimes synonymous with the comfortable life. All too often, our definition of success gets reduced to the comforts we can provide for ourselves. Success in life is seen as the ability to get a comfortable cup of coffee around the corner on the way to your comfortable job that affords you comfortable weekends.

I do not at all mean to be critical of an urban, domestic, or even a quiet life. What I do want is to push people to ask themselves—is the life I am living right now actually the right life for me? And if not, why am I still living it?

Almost always, the answer is because we are comfortable, and because we are scared of change and of the unknown. These feelings are natural and understandable. We all feel them; I know I sometimes do. But I refuse to let fear control my life. None of my goals would have been realized if I hadn't followed my heart and taken some pretty big risks in life. The success and happiness I have found in life have been hard won in the face of uncertainty and adversity that were of my own making. In that regard, I regret nothing.

I grew up in Catskill, New York. My four siblings, all went to work for the family business, and I started down the same road. I studied engineering in college, and upon graduation, I went to work for the family business too. I made a great salary with benefits right out of college.

I was also miserable. It took me only a few months to realize that working in New York was not the life for me.

Rather than stay miserable, I made a very difficult decision to leave my job, my family, and my entire life to go out west. I had been out to the West a few times for ski races, and so I decided that would be a great place to start my new life. I wanted a place that offered a sense of adventure, and a life that offered the same. Now I was going to go out and find it. I told my family that, after Christmas, I was moving to Salt Lake City.

When I got to Utah, I didn't know exactly what to do. My degree in mechanical design could have gotten me another job out there, but that wasn't why I had moved across the country. I ended up taking a job in a restaurant at the Snowbird ski resort. This provided me with a free ski pass and a little spending money.

I stress a *little* spending money. That first year in Utah was very hard on me financially and emotionally. I was broke all the time. I shared an old house just to make rent. By the time springtime rolled around, I was already running out of money. It became clear that, if I stayed at the house and continued paying rent, I would empty out my bank account completely. Before that happened, I decided to stretch what little savings I had left by moving into a tent in the woods.

I did this for six months. Every morning I would crawl out of my tent and go to work. After my shift, I would come back to my tent in the woods. It was a hard time. It was a scary time. I had succeeded in one thing though—this was about as uncomfortable as I had ever been! But not in the way I had planned. This was not what I had signed up for. This was outside my comfort zone, but it was also beneath my expectations for myself.

I decided then that I would not settle for this life. I wouldn't just be a ski bum forever. I wanted to do something different from a service industry job. I wouldn't accept being broke and homeless. I was going to push myself to do better and be better. No one was going to provide anything for me, nor did I want anyone to. My life was my own responsibility, and I was going to take responsibility and push myself as far as I could.

But how? What would I do? I didn't want to work in restaurants forever, but I also didn't want to be a ski instructor or a race coach.

What did pique my interest was ski patrol. The Snowbird Ski Resort is in one of the most avalanche-prone canyons in the country. I was fascinated by rescue work and patrolling. I decided to get my EMT medical certification. I landed a trail crew job at Snowbird, moved up into ski patrol, and later became an avalanche forecaster.

I am now in my twenty-third year on ski patrol. I have also done twenty years of rescue work with Wasatch Backcountry Rescue, an organization I headed for twelve years. I have guided treks and climbs all across the globe, and nine years ago I started my own trekking company, World Wide Trekking. I also founded a non-profit devoted to giving back to the community. And I am far from done in life.

None of this would have been possible if I hadn't told myself that I wasn't going to accept failure. None of it would have been possible if I hadn't been willing to push myself out of my comfort zone again and again and again. It wouldn't have been possible if I hadn't been willing to proceed despite fear and discomfort. It definitely wouldn't have been possible if I hadn't set a higher standard for myself and pushed myself to measure up to it.

My achievements are huge to me, but by other standards they are perhaps humble. That's fine by me. My life has been one long competition with myself. I don't compete with others, but I am always in direct competition with myself, pushing myself harder, setting a higher standard for myself. And as a guide, I work to push other people harder, too. As a guide, I find success in other people's achievements.

This book is part of my story.

Now I would like to know—would like you to know—what is yours? What do you want to accomplish in life, and what are you doing to make it happen? Are you willing to go outside your comfort zone to make it happen?

Chapter One

Mt. McKinley:
Acceptable and Unacceptable Risks

"If you're going through hell, keep going."
—Winston Churchill

After finishing my bachelor's degree in mechanical design in 1992, I went to work for the family business. I was twenty-two years old. Within about six months I realized that that life was not for me. I quit my job and moved out west to Utah. I worked in the mountains and spent all my time skiing, climbing, camping, and exploring the mountains. I climbed all over the Rockies, but soon I was hungry for bigger challenges and new adventures. I was ready to set my sights higher—*much* higher. On Mt. McKinley to be exact.

> **McKinley rises to a summit of 20,237 feet— the highest elevation in North America.**

Climbing in the Rocky Mountains had taught me much about climbing, but nothing in Utah could have prepared me fully for McKinley. Also known as Denali, McKinley is part of the Alaska Range. The mountain rises to a summit of 20,237 feet—the highest elevation in North America, and a good 6,000 feet higher than anything in Utah. McKinley is famous for having the greatest base-to-peak rise of any mountain in the world that is entirely above sea level. This gives McKinley a stature like no other mountain.

McKinley was my first big, committed, multi-day climb. It would be one of the great adventures of my life. Two of my good friends, Rob Moore and Mike Morris, came along with me. We were a small team of friends on the adventure of our lives. We were all young (I was about twenty-five at the time) and ready for adventure. We had saved hard for this trip, and I was now completely broke. I had spent the entire winter saving up money from my ski patrol job in Utah in order to pay for my plane tickets, gear, and climbing permits. When the time finally came to go, we were eager and full of drive. We were ready to face the mountain.

We flew to Anchorage and took a bus from there to the village of Talkeetna. From there, we took a small ski plane up the mountain. The pilot brought us down on the glacier and confirmed that he would be back in a month to pick us up. Then he waved goodbye, and we watched the plane disappear into the sky.

It was then that it hit me that we would be there for a *full month*! We stopped to look around. The three of us were alone, with the Alaskan mountain range spread out around us. I had never been in such a hazardous environment before, certainly never for so long. The air was cold, the glaciers large, the weather extreme, and the crevasses many and deep. I was not scared, though—I was excited.

We had come prepared. We had our backpacks and another fifty pounds of gear on a sled. We wore harnesses so that we could rope up to one another as well as to the sled. The rope kept us bound together—literally and in spirit. It also kept us safe. If someone were to fall into a crevasse, the others would arrest the fall by driving our ice axes into the glacier. Roping together can be tricky. You have to keep the rope free of excess slack at all times so that, if someone does fall, you don't get yanked too hard and pulled down, too. Keeping the rope taut as you move is a skill. When you slow down, the rope tugs you. If you go too fast, you get slack that needs to be tightened up. You have to learn to move together as one on the mountain, everyone spread out, but careful to move together and keep the rope free of slack. This means that every step you take is a group effort.

It took us several days to make it up to the Base Camp trudging up the mountain in this way. We were climbing alpine style, carrying all of our own gear and dealing with everything on our own. Some people consider alpine style the purest form of mountain climbing because you are up there making it on your own, as a team, with no hired help to carry gear. Most climbers hire Sherpas to help them carry gear in the Himalayas, but no such help is readily available in the United States. We didn't mind carrying our own gear. We liked the sense of adventure that climbing this way inspires.

We had some setbacks early on, as you do on any climb. While making our way up the Kahiltna Glacier, we were camped at 11,000 feet when the first of several snowstorms hit us, dumping three feet of snow in two days. We were tent-bound for three days. Every hour or so—and sometimes every few minutes when the snow was falling hard or the wind was blowing snowdrifts over us—one of us had to exit the tent and dig it out of the snow to keep us from getting buried alive.

When the snow eventually quit, we were finally able to pack up and head higher. From there, we made our way up Motorcycle Hill and then Squirrel Hill on our way to Windy Corner at 13,500 feet, where we planned to cache gear[1] before stopping at the camp at 14,200 feet.

Windy Corner is a small pass in a valley on McKinley. The valley acts as a funnel for the winds, which pick up speed as they come down the mountain. The narrowness of the valley creates an airflow bottleneck at Windy Corner that can result in very high winds.

Windy Corner should always be traversed with care, but it was particularly unsafe when we approached. Another bad storm rolled through that day, turning Windy Corner into *Very* Windy Corner—*Treacherously* Windy Corner. There was no way we could forge ahead. The wind speeds were easily exceeding 70 mph, and we were being pelted with small pebbles and ice chunks.

As the snow continued to fall, we set up an emergency camp between the official camps. We barely got our tent up in the storm. The wind filled the tent with snow as we dove inside. We couldn't light our stove to melt snow for water or cook food. We just had to wait out the night the best we could. The winds howled all night. Snow came down furiously.

The weather was making the trip very difficult, even dangerous. Unbeknownst to us as the time, there had been an accident higher on the mountain that day. A climber had fallen, along with a climbing ranger who had gone up to help. It was a good thing we had waited out the storm lower on the mountain. We likely wouldn't have had anyone to rescue us if we had also gotten into trouble at the same time.

We survived the night in our tents, and the morning brought sun and good weather with it. We packed up and continued around Windy Corner without incident. At this point, we stopped to cache

---

1 As we move higher on the mountains it gets to steep and the altitude make it to difficult to tow the sled with our gear. We bury a cache of our gear then ascend up to the higher camp then in the following days we return to the cache and retrieve our gear and we carry a second load up to the higher camp to get all of our gear into position. This also aids in acclimatization.

supplies by burying them in the snow near Windy Corner, a common strategy on McKinley. We marked the spot with a wand[2] and continued on our way. We were headed up higher on the mountain, where we would drop more gear, then turn back to pick up what we had left at Windy Corner. This is a mountaineering technique common to alpine-style climbing that makes carrying heavy loads manageable as you move into higher, more difficult altitudes.

This method also helps with the acclimatization process. Each time you go higher and then come back down and rest, you get a little more acclimated to the low oxygen. McKinley is especially harsh when it comes to altitude sickness because you feel the altitude worse the farther you are from the equator. Just as there is no uniform sea level, there is no uniform atmospheric pressure throughout the world. The lowest layer of Earth's atmosphere, the troposphere, is thicker at the equator (ten miles) than at the poles (five miles) So the further you go from the equator, the lower the air pressure will be at any given altitude. McKinley is situated way up in Alaska not far from the Artic Circle, making it very hard on climbers. It is also cold, and the humidity is relatively high because the mountain borders coastal waters.

After burying our gear, we made our way up to the advanced Base Camp, (Camp IV) a small tent city at 14,200 feet, with climbers on expeditions from all over the world. We settled into Camp IV and spent the night there before going back to retrieve the gear we had left behind and bring it back up to camp. We had been up on the mountain for weeks now, and we were ready to make a stab at summiting. While we were happy to be on the mountain, we were beginning to get impatient with the weather. If another storm came in, we might be trapped in our tent again for several more days.

---

2 Mountaineers use wands to mark their routes. Wands are simply long, flagged rods that are embedded in the snow to be visible from a distance.

After spending the day building our camp, cutting snow blocks to build walls to protect us from the wind and snowstorms. We retired to our tent exhausted and melted snow into water to make hot drinks and food. This would be our Base Camp, and our highest camp for the rest of our month on the mountain. After a long week, we rested in our tent.

Half of the people who attempt to climb McKinley during any given year never summit, usually due to no fault of their own. The most common reason for not summiting is inclement weather conditions. I did not want this to happen to us. We had so much invested in this trip, both financially and emotionally. We had saved and scrimped for so long, and just to get to this point we had to do everything on the cheap. Our packs were full of Ramen noodles on which we were subsisting, and I had emptied my bank accounts for the plane ticket. With so much scarce, hard-earned money committed to the endeavor, I was emotionally invested in making this, my first big climbing trip of this caliber, a success. I wanted to summit, and I didn't want the weather denying us.

We left camp and headed out for the summit. We took the West Rib Cutoff route, which is a direct shot up from the camp at 14,200 feet straight to the summit ridge. We had made it up onto the summit ridge, but not all the way to the top, when the weather turned bad again and we were forced back down to Camp IV at 14,200 feet. The winds and blowing snow were too much, and the decision was made to turn back. It was a tough decision to make, but the level of risk was too high—unacceptably high—and turning back was the right thing to do.

We spent another three days tent-bound at high camp while the bad weather continued. When the storm finally moved out, we were eager to get going again—we didn't know how long the good weather would hold. Another storm might blow through at any time, and we would be stuck in our tents yet again.

For our second attempt at the summit, we took a different route, this time going up the west buttress. In order to move faster this time, we decided to travel light. We took minimal gear. We also decided not to rope up during our summit push. Without heavy packs and the rope weighing us down, we moved much faster this time. Our plan was to ascend quickly from Camp IV at 14,200 feet, up past the last camp at 17,000 feet, and then continue swiftly to the summit at 20,237 feet.

We headed out early in the morning and began climbing the headwall, which is the steepest part of the route and reaches a fifty-five-degree slope in places. Partway up the headwall, Rob called out to Mike and me.

"I'm going back!" he hollered through cupped hands. He was still exhausted from the push a few days earlier, and hadn't recovered due to the altitude. Mike and I convened to discuss what to do. We decided we would continue up without him. We felt good. The weather was holding right now, and we felt like we had a good chance of making the summit with minimal risk. Rob descended back to camp alone. Mike and I continued up the mountain.

The good weather continued to hold. This made for great climbing and enabled us to make a relatively quick ascent, as we had planned. Of course, we still paced ourselves, moving steadily, one step and then another, all the way to the summit. Climbing requires you to find a pace that works for you, both physically and mentally, so that you don't wear out or shock your body. You have to get into the right mental space. That's the only way to go up a mountain of this magnitude. You don't run up the mountain. You don't attack the mountain. You sneak up on the mountain. You set your pace and climb slowly and steadily, one foot in front of the other.

We made our way further up the headwall, past the camp at 17,000 feet and around Denali Pass, and started the final ascent to the summit. There is a final summit ridge at the top of the mountain that rises three hundred feet vertically to the peak. We made our way slowly up this ridge, coming closer and closer to the summit. Around us, the view was beautiful. The view from near the top of McKinley is impressive because of its base-to-summit ratio. There are no major secondary peaks or smaller mountains and peaks by this summit peak. The other mountains are far off in the distance, typically just barely poking out from beneath the clouds far below. This really gives you a sense of just how high you are.

Then the worst happened—the weather turned again, just as we were nearing the summit. The storm blew in quickly, nailing us when we were maybe only a hundred feet from the top. This may not sound like far, but at these altitudes, it can take an hour to cover that much ground. Meanwhile, the storm exploded around us. High winds. Blowing snow. Reduced visibility. The wind picked up and whipped at us furiously. The temperature crashed, and it was now easily −20°F, and windy.

At this point Mike and I had a decision to make—continue forward or turn back. We weighed our options, and the consequences and risk tied to those options. Whenever you go into a hostile environment, such as a high-altitude mountain, you are accepting a certain level of risk. Almost anything you do in life involves some level of risk. The question is—how much risk are you willing to accept? Sound decision-making is just a matter of analyzing and weighing that risk. There are acceptable risks and there are unacceptable risks. Each person has to decide for themselves which is which.

Going up on McKinley was a risk—climbing any big mountain is—but for me it was an acceptable level of risk. We knew when to stop and fall back or hunker down in our tent if the weather turned bad. This was to mitigate risk, but we fully understood that one of the consequences of going up the mountain was encountering bad weather. This was something we considered an acceptable risk. We understood the danger. We also knew what to do when the worst happened.

But now things were different. This time we were near the top of the mountain. The altitude was much higher. We also would have had to cross the summit ridge to make the summit, and the ridge is prone to high winds. That wasn't a risk I was willing to take, and neither was Mike. We understood that the consequence of going up on the ridge could be the loss of our lives. That didn't seem worth it to us. Making this decision was difficult; we were so close, yet so far away. In the end, when we evaluated the conditions and considered the possible consequences of falling off the ridge, the decision was an easy one to make. The mountain wasn't going to let us up today.

This was a very hard decision to make after we had invested so much time, energy, and money into summiting. We were *so very close*. Nonetheless, continuing to plow ahead into the storm would have been an unacceptable risk. We knew that we could not let the summit blind us to this risk. There was nothing to be done but abandon the goal. It meant failing at summiting the mountain, but to do otherwise would have been to risk the ultimate failure, which on the mountain means not coming home.

Having made the decision to abandon our summit attempt, we turned back and started down in the middle of the storm. Our new goal was to forget the summit and focus on the second half of the journey—getting back down alive. We had placed wands on the way up to mark our path, spaced out fifty to two hundred feet apart, to make the descent safer and easier in case of weather like this. We now followed these to find our way off the mountain. Unfortunately, the wands were getting harder and harder to see as the winds picked up and blew snow around.

The temperature had dropped precipitously, and it was now easily −30°F. I stopped to put on my down pants and my big coat. By the time I had my warmer gear on, the visibility had basically dropped down to zero. Clouds had descended on us, and snow began falling and blowing in the wind. We went from being able to see thousands of feet down to a visibility of five hundred feet. Then down to a hundred feet, then fifty, then ten, then to complete blindness and vertigo.

It was at this point that I realized I had lost Mike. Because we were not roped together, I had no way to know where he was. I called out to him repeatedly, but heard no answer. Either he couldn't hear me over the winds, or I couldn't hear him—or both. Not only could I not find my partner, I also realized I couldn't find the next wand. I started crawling down the mountain in a sea of white. I could barely even see my hand in front of my face at some points, much less the wands. It had all happened so fast—I felt blindsided.

At this point, I started to get scared. I was angry at myself for having put myself into this situation. I was at 20,000 feet on a brutally cold mountain in a hostile environment, alone, separated from my partner. There was no one to blame for my predicament but myself, which is exactly what I did. I kept thinking—*You blew it,*

Dean! Great job. You're going to freeze to death on this mountain on your hands and knees. I thought about my family, my mother back at home having to hear the news, and my mind raced.

I took a deep breath. Negativity was getting the best of me. I needed to pull it together. How I had gotten into this situation didn't matter then. I was there, and it was up to me to step up and get myself down off the mountain. No one was going to save me. Sometimes these things happen, and sometimes they happen quickly. There was no reason to blame myself for pursuing a hobby I loved despite the inherent risks involved. The situation had changed for the worse, but there was nothing to do but face it head on. I had gotten myself into a bad situation, but I wasn't about to give up. You don't give up, no matter how bleak things look. I often tell my groups, when the mountain pushes you, *push back*! In this environment, throwing up your hands and lying down means lying down to die. If I had stopped and just waited there I would certainly have frozen to death.

I continued to press forward blindly. I was down on my hands and knees, feeling my way down off the glacier. Since I couldn't see the wands, I felt for the footprints we had left in the snow on our way up. I ran my fingers over the glacier, feeling for where our crampons[3] had scarred it. It was hard to find our tracks with the snow blowing over the glacier, but I managed to locate each footprint, one after the other, running my hands over the glacier methodically. In this way, I slowly inched down off the mountain through the storm.

Bit by bit, I made my way down, feeling out the way in front of me. I crawled down the mountain, alone, cold, blinded, literally on my hands and knees. I edged along like this, feeling for the crampon

---

3 A crampon is a metal plate with spikes fixed to a boot used for secure travel on snow and ice, such as crossing glaciers, snowfields and icefields, ascending snow slopes, and scaling ice-covered rock.

marks, for what felt like hours, until I finally found the next wand. Success! Finding that wand felt better than summiting ever could have. I was now determined. I may not have made it to the summit, but I would still make it back down alive.

I went on like this for hours, crawling along, moving from one wand to the next as I made my way back to my tent at the camp. Eventually, I came across another lost climber, a Korean man. He came over to me, surprised to see someone else out in the storm, but happy to have found another human being. We both felt relieved not to be alone.

The Korean man had gotten separated from his expedition team and was lost too. I told him to follow me, and we continued down the mountain together. Helping him buoyed my own spirit and inspired me. Taking on responsibility for another person gives you motivation and gives you someone to hold you accountable. He was standing there, afraid to move, needing me to lead, and that inspired me to keep pushing on.

We made progress down the mountain. Yes, it was slow progress, down-on-our-hands-and-knees progress, but progress all the same. We crawled on through the snow. I was up front, the Korean climber close behind. Eventually, the clouds began to thin, the winds died down, and the snow stopped blowing as hard. Visibility improved, and I could now see Mike up ahead of me. He wasn't even all that far away, only a couple hundred feet, but we hadn't been able to hear each other over the howling winds. The storm had both blinded and deafened me, robbing me of my two best senses and forcing me to find my way down the mountain by feel alone.

The three of us made our way down to the camp at 17,000 feet. At this point, the Korean climber reconnected with his team. I never saw him again after that event. We never spoke a word, using only hand gestures throughout the incredible experience we went through together. Mike and I continued back down to Camp IV together.

We never did end up summiting on that trip, but by making sound decisions, we had saved our own lives. I realized up there that it isn't just about getting to the top—it's about getting up and back down again. This is something I remind everyone I guide now—my job is to get them up to the top *and* back down safely. The summit, if you make it, is only the halfway point. You are still in a hazardous environment once you summit, often the most hazardous on the mountain, as was the case that day on McKinley. Most climbing accidents and deaths happen when coming off the mountain. It is easier to slip and fall when descending. Also, you are more tired and worn out on the descent, sometimes even sick from the altitude. You're dehydrated and hungry. You can lose your focus.

Many climbers get obsessed with the summit. I know I was. This eagerness to get to the top can make people lose sight of the ultimate goal of staying alive. Don't be blinded by such goals, and be ready to abandon them as you need to. You have to be constantly aware of your situation on the mountain and always reassessing. No decision is firm. The whole time we were on McKinley, we were re-evaluating our situation. Sometimes, when the weather was bad, we fell back and stayed in our tents. We chose to stay on the mountain though, despite the risk, until we deemed the risk was too great, and at that point we turned and left.

This is how I make all big decisions. I weigh my options against the risk that I consider to be acceptable. I consider the potential consequences of each option and then make my decision and proceed. This isn't the end of the process, however. Once you make a decision and act on it, you have to face whatever consequences result from *that* decision. As consequences unfold and your situation changes,

> **In a dangerous environment, you are always taking in your surroundings, analyzing your levels of risk, and adjusting your plan as you go.**

you must continue to reassess. Good decision-making never ends. It's a process and a way of being, not an action. On a mountain you are constantly re-evaluating your situation and your decisions. In a dangerous environment, you are always taking in your surroundings, analyzing your levels of risk, and adjusting your plan as you go. Sometimes that means abandoning your goal of summiting, as we did near the top of McKinley, so that you don't have to pay the ultimate price of not coming home.

CHAPTER TWO

Mount Everest:
Goal-Setting Strategies to Everest and Beyond

"It is not the mountain we conquer, but ourselves."
—Sir Edmund Hillary

Summiting Everest remains the ultimate goal for many mountain climbers. Everest is the world's highest mountain, and one of its most extreme environments. No one decides to summit Everest on a whim. Reaching the world's highest peak is the culmination of a lifetime of training, years of preparation, and several months spent going up and down the mountain to acclimatize before finally pushing to the summit.

Because goals of this magnitude are daunting when taken as a whole, undertakings like Everest are best viewed as a series of smaller goals. Divide the ultimate goal into smaller task segments, and focus only on the segment before you. In the case of Everest, you start by preparing and training, which means climbing a variety of smaller mountains (Denali, Aconcagua, Cho Oyu) first, building your skills and experiences, learning about altitude and camping out in the snow and cold, and learning how to deal with an unforgiving and uncomfortable environment. A lot of this is adopting the right mindset. You have to learn to be comfortable being uncomfortable.

Once you are actually on Everest, you break that climb into a series of smaller goals. You can't just fly to the landing strip, throw on your pack and harness, and make a beeline to Base Camp and then up to the top. No one can climb high mountains this way. From the landing strip, it is a ten-day trek to Base Camp, with thousands of pounds of gear and supplies in tow. For many people, the journey to Everest Base Camp is an adventure in and of itself, and it is a very popular trek. We trek up the lower Khumbu valley, going from village to village, staying in teahouses and lodges along the way, taking our time to slowly let our bodies adjust to the altitude as we go. Soon we leave the lush lower valley and enter the barren upper valley, and from there we make our way into Base Camp.

When you do get up on the mountain, you begin the long acclimatization process. First you must acclimatize to higher elevations, then come down and rest so that your body recovers before going back up a little bit higher next time. Each time you go up and down the mountain, your body acclimatizes a bit more. During this process you are moving your gear into position, and eventually, after however many weeks or months you need, you will also have moved yourself into a position to attempt the summit.

Conditions on Everest only permit a very short window of time during which you can actually make the summit. Most successful climbs happen in May. By early June, warmer temperatures can make the snow and ice unstable. Even in May, you have to wait for a window during which the jet stream (which can rage with wind speeds of over a hundred miles per hour) lifts above the mountain. To get to the summit, you have to position yourself at the right time, and even then you're still largely at the mercy of the weather. I had been planning to attempt Everest for many years by the time I actually made it to Nepal to do the climb. It was 2005, and I was thirty-five years old. I had spent years training for this opportunity, and now here I was in Nepal on an Everest climbing permit, and taking on the challenge as a guide.

To get to the top safely and with your sanity intact, you must surrender the idea of controlling what you cannot control. Do not dwell on that which you cannot do anything about. It is a waste of energy to worry about the possibility of weather or an avalanche, constantly asking yourself, What if?

You must understand that this doesn't mean you can ignore the weather or slope conditions; on the contrary, you actually have to pay even more attention to both of these dynamics as they relate to your controllable surroundings. You want to be totally aware of what is happening in the moment and not dwelling on abstract possibilities. You need to practice total situational awareness so that you can be attuned to changes in the weather and the mountain; this enables you to find your window and avoid mountain dangers. You have to come prepared with the right ropes, anchors, and other climbing gear and pay careful attention to their proper use. You should be hyper-aware of safety at all times. These are the things that you can control, and they should be the focus of your attention.

> **Summiting Everest is an expensive endeavor— guided expeditions cost upwards of $65,000 plus travel expenses, time and gear.**

One trap people fall into is being so focused on summiting that they abandon rationality and make bad decisions. Sometimes people push themselves too far, too high on the mountain, and run out of the time or energy that they need in order to safely get down off the mountain. Of course it's hard to walk away from a climb when you have invested so much time, energy, and money, but sometimes you must.

Summiting Everest is an expensive endeavor—guided expeditions cost upwards of $65,000 plus travel expenses, time and gear. My best hope for climbing Everest was to sign on with an existing expedition as a guide. My good friend Willie was the lead guide of an expedition for Mountain Madness, a guide and expedition company. Willie connected me with Christine, the owner of Mountain Madness, and she signed me on as a guide. I worked under Willie, and we worked under Christine, who joined us on the trip. Even going as a guide, the expedition was not free. The trip set me back tens of thousands of dollars I didn't have. Although I had saved as much as I possibly could for the trip, and several friends had donated to my efforts, I still had to put most of the bill on my credit cards. But it was worth it to me. I had tried to get on several previous expeditions, only to have the climbs fall through before we even got to Nepal. I had a chance now, and I wanted to take it, whether I could technically afford it or not. I wanted to make the climb so badly that I was willing to do whatever it took to make it happen.

We gathered in Kathmandu, assembled our gear, and flew in to Lukla landing strip in the lower Khumbu Valley to start our journey. It's a ten-day trek from the landing strip to Base Camp. We traveled each day from village to village, staying in teahouse lodges along they way. It is an amazing cultural journey, set amid the massive mountains in the high Himalayas. This is where you begin the long process of acclimatization.

After the long trek into the Khumbu valley we arrived at Mount Everest Base Camp, a barren landscape of ice and rock rubble with teams from more then fourteen countries. This is when you really learn about segmenting the climb into smaller goals. We began positioning ourselves and our gear for the summit, which we would not see for months. From Base Camp, we took gear and fuel up to Camp I, stayed the night to acclimatize, and then went back down to Base Camp for more gear and some rest. Over the next two months we went up and down the mountain in this way many times. Summiting Everest one time means climbing the mountain five or ten times (or more) as you scoot your gear up the mountain and cycle between acclimatization and coming down to rest and recoup.

I put the summit out of my mind and focused on getting from one camp to the other, up and back down again, up and back down again, my mind focused only on the task at hand. This was the only way I could keep myself in the right headspace to stay positive and stay safe.

The other crucial component to keeping your head in the right place is to accept that you are going to face setbacks along the way. You cannot let yourself get frustrated when something happens, or when the weather takes a turn for the worse. This is what I mean by focusing only on what you can control, not what you can't. So expect and accept setbacks. Instead of allowing yourself to become frustrated by them, focus on managing them.

My first setback on Everest came in the form of dental troubles. When we reached Camp II at 22,000 feet, the altitude made one of my molars start to hurt. An air bubble under a filling was expanding due to the low air pressure. I tried to tough it out, but I soon realized that I was going to have to take care of the tooth before continuing. Rather than getting frustrated about the situation, I resolved to take care of it so I could continue.

I split off from the expedition and descended down to Base Camp, and then made the two-day trek to Namche Bazaar, a village with a Sherpa dental clinic—which, at 11,800 feet, is the highest dental clinic in the world. The clinic is run by Nawang, a Sherpa woman trained as a dental hygienist. She drilled out the filling, relieving the pressure in my tooth. I then hiked two more days back to Base Camp, rested for a day, and then headed back up the mountain. I lost a week of climbing time, but it was a setback that couldn't have been avoided.

After returning from the dentist, I went back up and rejoined the expedition at Base Camp. The following day, we all went from Base Camp up to Camp II at 22,000 feet. The day after that, while the team was still at Camp II, I went back down to Camp I to retrieve some gear. I started down toward Camp I early that morning, and by mid day I was at Camp I and settled in with a load of gear to bring up to Camp II. I had originally planned to stay the night at Camp I by myself, but after being away from the team for so long down off the mountain, I was eager to rejoin the others. After retrieving my gear, I went straight back up to Camp II.

This turned out to be a very good decision. The mountain picked up fresh snow that night, and in the morning the snow came down in an avalanche that took out all of Camp I. Seven people who were using the camp were taken out by the avalanche. They were lucky to have been on the fringes of the avalanche, which kept anyone from getting killed, but they were all injured and had to be evacuated, ending their climb abruptly.

Had I stayed in Camp I the previous night, I too would have been hit by the avalanche. I remember looking down at Camp I in the morning and ruminating on how easily I could have been killed. I have seen many people hurt and killed in the mountains, and I realized that it could easily have been me as well. This thought unnerved me, so I pushed it from my mind. Dwelling on what could have been will just undermine your confidence and distract you from the things that you can and must control in real time.

I put yesterday's avalanche out of my mind and focused on the current conditions. We looked at the weather report and tried to judge the environment. We had planned to ascend from Camp II up the Lhotse Face to Camp III that night, but the avalanche hazard was too high because it had snowed all night. Ultimately, we decided to pack up and retreat back to Base Camp. Having been denied passage up to Camp III, we went back down to Base Camp to rest and then try again.

We needed to let the snow settle for a week before trying to ascend again. This caused one of the people in our expedition to quit and go home. He couldn't imagine going back up the mountain yet again. I understood how he felt; mentally, it is tough on you. But I also knew that this was all part of the process. You have to take everything as it comes. I wasn't focused on how many times I would have to go up the mountain, only on the one thing I needed to do next. All I knew was that I needed to give the snow some time to settle, which meant taking a week, resting, and gaining strength before pushing on. I wasn't thinking about the summit.

After resting for a week, we went back up through the Khumbu Icefall again. This is one of the most dangerous parts of Everest outside of the death zone.[4] We had to be especially careful now (after the snowfall) to watch for hidden crevasses and unstable snow packs. We crossed higher-hazard areas very carefully. To do this, you move slowly and steadily, without stopping. We stopped only for short breaks, and only in areas that had less exposure to the constantly shifting ice. Crossing hazardous areas is a matter of moving methodically and resting in islands of safety as you go. In these situations, it is important to practice situational awareness and avoid focusing on what could happen if you mess up—that will just cause

---

4 The term *death zone* refers to altitudes above which the available oxygen is insufficient to sustain human life.

you to mess up. You need to focus on making good decisions about every move you make, and not let yourself be distracted by the consequences of a misstep.

I am not saying that you should be reckless. I am saying you need to free your mind from distractions, including things you cannot control, and stay focused on what you *can* control, like getting up early before the snow heats up and destabilizes, avoiding unsafe areas until the conditions improve, and moving quickly through high-hazard areas like the icefall.[5] You can't let your guard down, even for a second. An American climber from another expedition died on the Khumbu Icefall during our climb. He slipped, fell into a crevasse, and died. He had gotten careless and neglected to clip in. It was a tragedy, and an avoidable one at that.

After the icefall, we passed Camp I, which was still buried in snow from the avalanche. Expedition groups were still there trying to dig their camps and gear out from beneath the avalanche debris. The loss of their high-altitude gear could cost them their chance at the summit if it wasn't retrieved. Our team pressed on straight up to Camp II. We were better acclimated and moving faster now, especially after a week of rest, which just goes to show that resting and stopping to acclimate aren't really setbacks at all, but an essential and beneficial part of the process. We rested another day at Camp II with the plan of heading up the following day to Camp III, which was located on a small ledge at 24,500 feet.

Getting to Camp III means scaling Lhotse Face, a steep, 4,000-foot-tall mountain face of solid ice that glitters in the sun. There is no room for error here as you scale the ice face. Miss a clip

---

5 An icefall is a portion of a glacier characterized by rapid ice flow and a crevassed surface. Most glacier ice flows at speeds of a few hundred meters per year, but the flow of ice in an icefall can be measured in kilometers per year. This rapid flow causes the ice to fracture, which forms crevasses.

with your rope and fall, and you slide all the way to the bottom and die. We were near Camp III, three quarters of the way up Lhotse Face, when a storm came in. Clouds dropped down on us. The wind picked up. We had to decide whether to turn back again. We wanted to spend the night at Camp III, the final stage of acclimatization, before returning to Base Camp to rest in preparation for our summit push.

This rest is a necessary part of the acclimatization process. Any time you spend high up on the mountain makes you weaker. You don't fully recover, not even when you're resting. When you first ascend to higher altitudes, your body will compensate for a few hours: your heart rate increases, your respiratory rate and heart stroke volume[6] also increase. After a certain amount of time at high altitude, either your body adjusts to the elevation and lower air pressure and begins to oxygenate your blood, or you start to show signs of AMS (Acute Mountain Sickness); nausea, headache, fatigue, and dizziness are some of the common signs of AMS.

Unfortunately, the storm was denying us passage. These kinds of storms are dangerous when you are out climbing and not in your tent—they often cause people to get frostbite and lose fingers and toes. To avoid that, we turned back yet again and descended to Camp II, where we spent the night.

The inclement weather had denied us access to Camp III a second time now, but rather than get frustrated with the weather, we accepted the setback. We couldn't control the weather, only our reaction to it. Turning back meant we would have to descend all the way to Base Camp before making yet another try at Camp III.

We weren't alone in this struggle. No other team had summited Everest yet that year, even though it was almost May. Although I

---

6 Stroke volume is the amount of blood that your heart pumps with each beat.

hadn't conceded the season yet, other people on the expedition had had enough. At this point, two more people on the expedition gave up and went home. We only had one remaining paying guest out of the four who had originally joined us on the expedition. The rest of us stayed on though, determined not to let the setback deter us from pursuing our goal.

After descending to Base Camp, we spent a week there regaining strength. We then made our second attempt up to Camp III. We now had a much smaller climbing team, due to the people who had left and gone home. By now we were well acclimated to the mountain, and we pushed straight to Camp II on the first day. On the next day, we started out toward Camp III, but the weather again forced us to turn back around, and we spent another night at Camp II. This meant that we had to go all the way back down to Base Camp yet again and rest for yet another week.

We then made a third attempt at Camp III, now having been denied twice. On our third attempt, having done the climb a few times, we were now strong enough to go straight to Camp III in one day.

The next day finally brought a little serendipity. The weather cleared, and the skies were blue and bright. We enjoyed that day immensely, as we were able to go at our own pace and not worry. After so many setbacks and losing so many climbers, we needed that day to boost morale. Every time someone quits and goes home, or you hear about someone dying on the mountain, it really takes the wind out of your sails. This was especially true that year, when absolutely no one had been able to summit. To persevere, you have to be able to see the light at the end of the tunnel.

I find that I am better able to keep things in perspective and maintain my high spirits when I divide big goals (like climbing the world's highest mountain) into smaller segments, taking a few steps at a time. Instead of focusing on the whole mountain, I would set small goals that I could accomplish immediately. A goal might be as small as taking ten steps before taking a break. I would then try to gain strength and boost my morale by thinking fondly of family and friends, or maybe just counting down from three, before continuing again. This allowed me to break the whole climb into manageable steps. It's hard to focus on a grueling three-month endeavor; it's easy to focus on taking ten more steps.

That night we made it back to Camp III and set up camp. Christine and I shared a tent, and Willie and Eric shared a tent. We put our two tents close together, leaving only the smallest of gaps between them. We used our cook stoves to make hot soup and drinks in the vestibules to try to warm up. We were at 24,500 feet, and the overnight temperatures were well below zero. We slept with all of our warm clothes on, with our boots and gloves in the sleeping bags with us so that they wouldn't ice up due to the frozen sweat inside them. Ice crystals formed inside both tents from the condensation of our breath, but we tried to stay warm bundled up in our bags.

We were cold, but we had our hot soups and drinks, and there was a sense of magic in the air. We were again optimistic, our spirits buoyed by the beautiful night. From our camp, we had seen the sun set over Cho Oyu in the distance. Down below us, we could see the path we had taken to get this far. Our struggles were laid out below us, and our setbacks too. We could see where the avalanche had happened at Camp I. As a mountaineer, I was feeling extremely proud of myself to have made it this far.

The next morning we left our gear in place at Camp III and retreated all the way back to Base Camp with the intention of then coming back, now fully acclimatized, to make a try at the summit. But first we needed a bit of rest at lower altitudes.

Unfortunately, once we got back down to Base Camp, the weather turned on us again. A monsoon system had moved into the region, which often signals the close of the season. The monsoon weather pattern can shift the jet stream down onto the mountain, besieging it with treacherously high winds. We knew there would be plumes of snow blowing hundreds of feet into the air at the top of the mountain. Visibility would be low. The wind chill would be dangerous. There was no way we could go back up this year unless the jet stream shifted back up, which would take at least a week, if it happened at all.

It dawned on me that it would do us all good to get off the mountain for a while. There was no use being there when we couldn't possibly ascend. Leaving the mountain to go to the dentist had allowed me to recoup and come back in tiptop shape, and that seemed like the best use of my time now. It was preferable to hanging around Base Camp all dispirited. I went down to one of the villages in the valley with Eric, our last remaining guest. We spent time at the teahouses, where we ate and rested. We slept in real beds. It was nice to relax, away from Base Camp. We let our bodies regain lost strength. Our red blood cells built back up as our blood oxygenated. And when we returned to Base Camp a few days later, we were recharged and ready to climb the mountain again.

Unfortunately, the mountain wasn't ready for us. High winds continued to blow on Everest for the next two weeks. This was an incredibly difficult time mentally, but we tried to make the best of the situation. We couldn't control the winds, so there was no use getting upset when they blew. Instead, we focused on what we could control: staying fit, active, prepared, and mentally ready.

Idleness is bad for morale in a situation like that, so I thought up ways to be busy. Willie and I used the time to train the Sherpas in CPR, and then in first aid and medical assessment. Sherpas from other camps came to take part in the trainings, and we happily trained them too. The second week we went up onto the icefall and did mock rescue drills. We lowered people into crevasses (simulating falls) and then staged "rescue" operations.

All this training was good for the Sherpas, climbers, and the other guides—but it was also good for me. It allowed me to be in control of the situation. By staying active and useful, I was able to keep my mind off the weather, which we couldn't control. Some of the other climbers didn't understand why we would go up in the icefall and train like this rather than just resting up, but staying busy and active actually helped keep us energized and ready. When the time came to summit, we would be physically and mentally ready for the undertaking.

There was one hitch though: it was getting late in the season. We had already been twice prevented from ascending the Lhotse Face, and we could easily be turned back again on our summit push. It was now late May. All permits expire in early June, because by June the days get too warm, causing the mountain snow and ice to become less stable and unsafe. If we were going to summit, it had to be soon. We checked the weather forecasts religiously.

Finally, in late May, there were a few *potential* windows, so we started to get ourselves back into position on the mountain in Camp II, hoping one of the windows panned out. The last thing we wanted was to be waiting at Base Camp when the season expired. It was disheartening down there. There were fewer and fewer people, as climbers and whole teams gave up and left, thinking Everest wasn't going to let anyone up that year. Every time another team of climbers gave up and left, we felt more discouraged.

We made our push up the mountain. We knew we probably wouldn't have another opportunity, so this was now or never. When we made it to Camp II, the weather was still bad. The winds were still high. But we kept hoping conditions would clear once we were in position. We set up camp for the night, but started making plans to leave the following day if the weather didn't get better.

That night, I was restless in my tent. A storm blew over and I lay in my tent listening to the thunder roll and watching the lighting flash. The situation was frustrating and emotionally draining. I kept asking myself why the weather wouldn't give us a break and let us up. It made me feel out of control. While it is best to avoid focusing on things you can't control, doing so is easier said than done. I didn't know if the mountain was going to give us favorable conditions and let us up. You can't fight against the bad weather and the wind and the cold temperatures and storms. It was a terrible feeling. I had put a lot of time, energy, and money into this climb, and I was starting to doubt we would make it.

But what really upset me was my own thinking. There was no reason to be so negative. We had done all we could, and now we had to accept the mountain on its terms. There was no reason for me to lie in my tent feeling like a failure. We had done our best, and all we could do now was keep going.

The next morning, we woke to see the clouds retreating up the South Col, the canyon between Everest and Lhotse Face. The weather and wind were retreating! We decided to try for the summit after all. That day, we pushed straight up to Camp III again. We spent the night at Camp III, and in the morning we started to use supplemental oxygen set to a low flow. I had just a few bottles of oxygen, which I needed to ration so that they would last me all the way to the summit and back.

We pushed on toward Camp IV. Even with the oxygen, the altitude at this height is hard on your body. The atmospheric pressure on top of Everest is three times lower than at sea level, which means each breath gives you only a third of the oxygen you need. Your heart races, even at rest. Your body begins to move more slowly. Each step is a struggle through a very hostile environment. Even your wits begin to leave you. That high up on the mountain, moving a mile can take even a strong climber twelve hours. This is where you have to really focus on the moment. Your goal is no longer getting to the top—it's putting the next foot forward. Each step is an arduous task. Even with supplemental oxygen, the death zone is still taxing. We only had a few bottles for each person, and we had to keep the flow low to avoid running out.

> The atmospheric pressure on top of Everest is three times lower than at sea level, which means each breath gives you only a third of the oxygen you need. Your heart races, even at rest.

Luckily, the good weather was holding out. The winds had shifted higher up the mountain. We could still see snow plumes above us on the summit ridge, but down on South Col the weather had lifted enough to allow us to continue up. We realized this was it—we were making our push at the summit, the last one we could possibly squeeze in this year before the window closed. The weather was still bad on the summit, and we might have to turn around near the top, but we were making the push anyway.

We worked our way above the Yellow Band, a strip of rock that appears yellowish due to its marble content, and the Geneva Spur, an anvil-shaped outcropping (named by the Swiss in 1952) that must be scaled. We slowly made our way to Camp IV at 26,000 feet, just inside the death zone. Entering the death zone makes you feel simultaneously lethargic and excited, and I was excited to be near the top after so many months of climbing.

The environment is extreme, however. Practicing situational awareness becomes more critical, but also more difficult. The lack of oxygen is so extreme above the death zone that the brain and body get starved for oxygen. Your mind and body begin to move slowly.

We arrived at Camp IV at about two o'clock in the afternoon and put up our tents. The three Sherpas and I had decided to bring just one tent and two sleeping bags for the four of us. We'd left the rest at Camp III to lighten our load. The four of us all huddled together for warmth that night, sharing a tent with two men to a bag. Willie, Christine, and Eric shared a second tent. We were crowded but warm, even though the temperatures were subzero outside.

That afternoon we had a meeting and decided to rest up a few hours before heading out for the summit later that evening. We spent the rest of the afternoon caring for ourselves. We tried to sleep. We forced down food even though the altitude had wrecked our appetites. All we could keep down were potato chips and other fatty junk food. I washed and dried my feet and put on the pair of clean socks I had been saving the whole trip for just this moment.

At seven o'clock in the evening, we got up and made hot drinks and got ready to head out for the summit. I forced down hot tea and Tang to hydrate and got myself ready to go. We were moving so slowly due to the altitude that it took us two hours to get ready to set out. Our bodies were beginning to wither away, and we knew we couldn't stay in the death zone for long.

By nine o'clock that evening, we were on our way to the summit, hoping the mountain would let us up. We were excited, but we remained mindful that no one else had made it up this far that year, so we were the first ones to set the lines and the rope to the top. We moved slowly, conserving energy, careful not to overexert ourselves.

We were slowly pushing up toward the Balcony,[7] then up the ridge toward the south summit, where we would make our last dash to the summit. We could hear thunder and see lightning from far-off storms, but the skies over Everest were clear. We were excited to see that we really did have a chance at the summit. Moonlight illuminated the mountains around us, lighting up several of the other eight-thousand-meter peaks. We could see both Makalu and Lhotse in the distance. As the light of day began to dawn, we were level with those peaks, themselves some of the highest mountains in the world.

The light started creeping up over the mountains as we neared the top, which had been our plan all along. This gives a spectacular view of the Himalayas because summiting in the early morning puts the warmth of the sun on your back just as you hit the highest elevations (where the air is at its absolute coldest). The air temperature had hovered around forty below zero while we climbed overnight. Although we were wearing full down suits meant for climbing above 8,000 meters, we were cold in the thin, biting air.

At the Balcony, we changed out oxygen bottles. I had brought three bottles in all. This was my second. I hid the third one in the rocks so that I wouldn't have to carry the weight to the top. Making

---

7 The Balcony is a small platform at 27,600 feet where climbers can rest.

sure to remember where I had hidden the bottle, we continued to ascend the mountain. One of the last hurdles is the Hillary Step, the last cliff leading to the summit. This is a challenging climb due to the sheer exhaustion of being well above 8,000 meters. Despite the altitude, I was actually feeling pretty good. The low oxygen combined with my anticipation was making me feel euphoric. The good weather was also buoying my spirits. When we got up over the Hillary Step and started traversing the south ridge to the summit, it hit me: *We were going to make it.* My mind raced. I thought about my family and friends. I thought about the times I had wanted to quit and turn back, and how by having pressed on, I would now get to stand on top of the world. My suffering faded into the background as it began to sink in that I was about to realize a major life goal. After so many months on the mountain, so many small goals meant to get us nearer to the top, here we were on the summit ridge.

The next goal: the summit itself.

Finally, at 9:30 a.m., we made it. We were literally on top of the world. Mount Everest. By the time we reached the summit, we had been climbing for twelve and a half hours. We were standing at 29,035 feet above sea level. All of the Himalayan Mountains were at our feet, spread out in every direction. It was simply amazing. We took photos, of course, with the cameras that we had tucked into our suits so that they wouldn't freeze. But no photo can really do it justice. No panoramic shot can capture the true scale.

We were the first party to make it to the top of Everest that year, but many more followed. As we climbed the south ridge, I could see another team coming up over the north ridge from China at the same time. We all stayed at the summit for a half hour or so, and I did a lot of thinking about all the challenges we had overcome and the countless little goals that had been set and met in order for us to stand on top of the world.

Unfortunately, we couldn't dally. We still had to get down, and it was best to do so while we still had daylight. Most accidents happen on descent, so we needed to be extra careful to avoid making any mistakes. Our party was eager to start. Getting back down takes days, and we had already had a long day. We had been climbing at super-high altitudes for over twelve straight hours to get to the summit, and we would need time to get back down to Camp IV. Before heading out, I took one last look out at the highest mountain range in the world from its highest peak, knowing that I was looking down at the rest of the world.

Then we were on our way back down. When we got back to the Hillary Step, we had to wait in line to use the ropes that we had set to rappel down the cliff. Climbing teams coming up behind us were using our ropes, which would have been fine, except they kept clipping in to come up before letting us go down. We shouted at people to let us come down, but they just kept hooking in, and once someone was hooked in, we couldn't rappel down without crashing into them.

After waiting forty freezing cold minutes, one of us finally made the move and clipped into the rope when one of the ascending climbers was five feet from hooking in but too exhausted to lunge for the rope himself. One of us rappelled down and then kept people from hooking into the rope until we had all reached the bottom.

You cannot let your guard down on the descent. The descent is always dangerous if you aren't careful. Everyone was tired and eager to get down now that they'd already summited. We were dehydrated and hadn't slept well in days. Summiting is a great accomplishment, but it's only half of the goal—you still have to get back down. You have to keep reminding yourself to pay attention to your surroundings, stay aware, and focus on the last leg of the trip. You have to keep your wits about you, even as your brain is starving for oxygen. We had anticipated this and hidden some oxygen canisters down below the cliff. It took me a while to remember where I had put them, but we finally found them and hooked up to fresh oxygen.

We passed other climbers all day as we descended. Finally, by late afternoon, we had made it back to Camp IV. We again crowded into two tents and struggled to sleep. This was my third night with no sleep at all. I was exhausted, but completely unable to sleep at such high altitudes. Still, I lay there trying to rest and recover. But mostly I glowed, basking in our success.

In the morning we descended over steep rock areas from Camp IV to Camp III. You still can't fall—or even slip—or it's all over. We were weighed down terribly because we had to bring all our gear off the mountain, and we still hadn't recovered from being in the death zone for almost two days. We took a break at Camp III and loaded all our gear onto our backs, then descended down the Lhotse Face with all of this extra weight and our bodies badly beaten. We spent another restless night at Camp II, where we loaded even more gear onto our backs.

The last major challenge was our final descent across the icefall. This would be our most dangerous passing because of all of the extra weight we were carrying, and because we were moving slowly and it was now June, which meant the icefall was more prone to collapsing due to the rising temperatures. With great patience, we descended the icefall one final time without incident. Then it was down to Base Camp, through the Khumbu Valley, and then back to the landing strip. We were so acclimatized and eager to get home that we made the trek out, which had taken us ten days coming onto the mountain, in only two days. In Kathmandu we spent a few nights celebrating with the team and the Sherpas before flying home.

The entire trip took almost three months. From the time I left Salt Lake City, it would be sixty-seven days before I summited, and I did not arrive back home for almost ninety days. Those three months changed my life, and will stay with me forever. The lessons I learned on Everest have stayed with me, and I use them every day: setting a series of small goals as a process to accomplish big goals, filtering out distractions and practicing situational awareness, focusing only on the things you can control, and learning to accept setbacks—all these practices aid me in my everyday life. They worked on Everest, and now they work for me in business and contribute to the work I do on my nonprofit, each and every day I am alive.

CHAPTER THREE

Carstensz Pyramid:
The Not-So-Reluctant Leader

Challenges are what make life interesting, and
overcoming them is what makes life meaningful."
—Joshua J. Marine

What was perhaps my strangest climbing adventure occurred on Carstensz Pyramid when I was forty-one years old. The mountain is in a remote section of Indonesia where even getting to Base Camp is a challenge. You have to take a series of commercial flights into Indonesia, but to even get close to the mountain you have to take a bush plane to a dirt landing strip in the jungle. From there, it is a challenging, week-long trek through rain and mud, hacking your way through the jungle with a machete. You generally don't see any other climbers the whole time—I didn't—which underscores how isolated the area is.

I went as a private guide for a single guest, but we were on a permit with eight other climbers plus local help. After a week of seemingly constant rain, we arrived at Base Camp and set up our tents. I started to talk to the group about running training scenarios for being up on the mountain. Even though I only had one client, my practice is to include everybody in the training drills I run with all my clients, practicing ascending the fixed lines and passing anchors. Sharing knowledge is always a good thing to do, and I firmly believe you should get to know the people you climb with; drills facilitate that.

I also just wanted to help keep people safe. Carstensz Pyramid is a challenging climb. Steep jagged cliffs rise to the summit at 16,024 feet. You have to traverse crags as you move from one rock pinnacle to the next by ascending and shimmying across fixed ropes. I wanted to run some scenarios to make sure everyone was properly prepared.

Despite the challenge, the ascent went off without a hitch. We all made it to the summit, where we celebrated for about a half hour before starting back down the sheer cliffs. Eventually we got off the cliffs and headed back to Base Camp. Everyone was exhausted. We were tired, hungry, and thirsty. After a quick meal, everyone crawled into their tents and passed out almost immediately.

That night, in the early morning hours before sunrise, I was awakened by the sound of shouting outside my tent. The shouting was in Indonesian, so I knew it must have been one of our porters.

Not knowing that much of the local language, I couldn't tell what the commotion was about, so I got up to investigate. There was indeed a porter outside screaming at some of the other people on staff, who all stood a few feet back because the porter was brandishing a machete at them, swinging it menacingly. Thankfully, all the guests had stayed in their tents, but surely the noise had woken and frightened them.

"If one of us dies, one of you dies." We were still in a volatile situation.

"What's he saying?" I asked the other staff.

Someone leaned into me and whispered that he was shouting, "If one of us dies, one of you dies." The porter was just chanting this repeatedly.

Here was the situation: We had paid several porters to stay down lower on the mountain with our supplies while we went up to the summit. There had been an accident. While waiting for us to come back down, the porters had been staying in a cave, which partially collapsed on them when a large flake of rock came off the ceiling of the cave. One of them was hit in the head with a rock.

I didn't understand why this porter was taking it out on us. All I knew was that the situation needed to be de-escalated. I put my hands up nonthreateningly and tried to coax him into putting down the machete so we could get a translator and talk things out. Suddenly, the porter lunged at me. I jumped back and rejoined the group. A standoff ensued for an hour, with the porter pacing around our camp, shouting angrily. He continued to swing the machete around, occasionally smacking it against the ground. Then, all of the sudden, he grew quiet, lowered the blade, and headed back down the canyon.

We breathed a sigh of relief, but we still didn't know what to do. We retired to our individual tents, and I mulled the situation over. This was serious business. We were alone on the mountain. We hadn't seen any other climbing parties the entire time we were there; not a single soul. There was no place to run or hide, and we couldn't stay at Base Camp forever either. The climb was over, and we needed to head back, but getting back through the jungle without the help of the porters would have been nearly impossible. And yet, minimizing interaction with them seemed prudent, given that this was an isolated area of New Guinea outside the reach of local law and marked by tribal conflict. But we couldn't just stay in our tents forever, either.

The situation couldn't just be ignored. I was concerned that, if we did nothing, the porters would grow angrier, and then I didn't know what might happen. We needed to reach a mutual understanding and show them that we cared. I resolved to go down the mountain and meet with them. Two people on staff reluctantly agreed to accompany me. The rest of the staff stayed behind with the guests. The mood was very tense in camp, and everyone was scared to go down. I had reservations, but someone had to take ownership of the situation, and I let the task fall to me.

The three of us hiked several hours down the mountain to the cave where the porters were. There was an Indonesian man with a rifle standing outside the camp. We waved to him while making a slow approach. He stared at us coldly. I pointed at the camp, signaling our intention to come in, and when he made no move to stop us, we entered the camp.

Suddenly, one of the porters took me by the forearm. He led me deeper into the camp, one hand on a machete and the other on me. He took me to the body of a porter who lay on his back in the middle of the camp, a tarp draped over him head to toe like a shroud. Everyone stood around the body. The tension in their camp was palpable. The porters avoided eye contact with us, looking as nervous and uncomfortable as we were. They seemed surprised that we had shown up.

The porters then took me to the cave where the collapse had happened. They pointed to the spot where the cave had collapsed, and I could see where the rock had broken away and struck the porter. The rock still lay on the cave floor; it was large, and it was easy to see how it could kill a man. The porters started gesturing with their hands to take pictures of where the rock had fallen. I didn't understand why they wanted me to take photos, but I was willing to oblige. I took out my camera and snapped some photos of the cave and the rock for them.

We went back out to the body. There were women walking

about, crying mournfully. The men were still tense. Some stared vacantly into the distance. Others crouched in the corners of the camp, glaring at me. These were the ones I was most afraid of. They were quiet, but they looked ready to explode in anger. I knew someone needed to do something, but I was reluctant to get involved. If I pulled the tarp back and found the man there dead, was I then responsible for the situation? I wasn't sure I wanted that responsibility. Still, someone had to step up and do something. I went over to the body and peeled the tarp back. There was no external bleeding, but spinal fluid was seeping from the porter's ear, which signaled a skull fracture. To my utter surprise, however, his chest was rising and falling. I put my ear to his lips and could feel his breath. It wasn't a body at all. He was still alive!

I stood and backed up. "He's not dead."

They just stared at me, unable to tell what I was saying.

My mountain rescue instincts took over. Someone needed to take a leadership role and get these people moving. I often find that getting people involved and moving in an emergency or volatile situation helps to keep tension down because it gets everyone preoccupied and working together. There would be no time for violent conflict if we had to work together to do this rescue.

I pulled back the tarp and laid it out alongside the injured man and motioned for the porters to help me get him onto the tarp. I stabilized his head while the porters lifted him. We wrapped the tarp around him and used it to carry him down the valley to a nearby gold mine. This was the closest place to take him where we might be able to get help. It was one of the largest gold mines in the world, and I knew there would be security there, and possibly medical care. They would likely have medics on site for the miners, and maybe even a helicopter.

It was only a couple of hours away on foot. We trudged down the valley for hours, toting this gravely injured man on our makeshift stretcher, everyone working together to get him down to where we could hopefully find help.

As we approached the perimeter of the mining facilities, we were met by the local Indonesian security force in charge of protecting the mine—six men armed with automatic weapons. This was a huge open-pit mining operation with high-level security and a militarized protection force. Unbeknownst to us at the time, tensions were high on the mine because thousands of local Indonesian workers were striking and rioting.

We approached and set the injured man down on the ground at the top of a steep bank, near a large storage container (about 10x16') and a generator that was powering the lights that lit up the perimeter of the mine. There was a group of guards congregated there, and I rolled back the tarp for them to see. The locals did the talking so that I didn't have to struggle to explain the situation in a foreign language.

The guards called for an ambulance. We had to wait for quite some time, as the mine was huge, and it took a while for anyone to respond to the call. Eventually, an ambulance came. The mine medics checked his vitals and then loaded him into their land cruiser and took him away.

At this point I was feeling pretty good about what we had done—we had shown our goodwill and done everything we could to help the man. The two staff guys and I bid the porters goodbye and returned to our Base Camp. It was nearly dark when we got back, and everyone at camp was relieved to see us return safely, and eager to know what had happened. I related the story to them, and we discussed what to do next. We were still in a volatile situation.

At this point, one of the guests, a more experienced climber, nominated me for the informal position of group leader. This was partly because of the training exercises I had run earlier in our climb, but also because he understood that someone needed to take control of the situation, and he felt that the way I had handled the injured porter made me a good candidate. The rest of the group agreed by consensus. I was humbled by this vote of confidence and determined to get us out of there safely. This had been such an unexpected fiasco, not the kind of thing you plan for on a climb, but someone had to act as leader and help everyone get down safely.

My first action as leader was to have everyone in the group put their heads together and come up with a plan. Dictators don't make for effective leaders. Effective leaders understand that everyone has something to contribute, and that the best mind in a group is never as good as all the minds in a group combined. Leadership isn't about barking orders—it's about being a facilitator for decision-making. Good leaders work to bring groups together so that the sum of the group is greater than its parts.

We talked the situation over. We were still wary of going back through the jungle with the porters. The rescue had been a success, but we didn't really know what they were thinking or feeling. On the way through the jungle to the mountain, they had gone on strike several times and demanded a wage increase. I worried that we might go back with them and get a few days into the jungle only to have them turn on us and strand us in the middle of nowhere. I was also hesitant to show my face at the village where we had started our trek: We had stopped there to hire the porters on the way up the mountain. Who knew how the villagers might react when we returned minus one of their own.

As a group, we decided to return to the gold mine because it was the nearest sliver of modern civilization. The plan was to surrender to the mine company. We figured that, since they knew about the injured porter and the accident, we could explain the situation and ask for a rescue. They might be willing to take us back to the airport in Timika. That would spare us from being stranded in the jungle or getting into a conflict with the villagers.

We set out back through the long valley to the mine, traveling through rain and dense fog that took the visibility down to less than a hundred feet. We arrived back at the perimeter of the mine. There were signs everywhere to deter trespassers, but we didn't have any other options, so we passed the signs and continued up the steep bank where I had previously taken the injured porter to the mine security guards. We stopped near the storage container and the generator and assembled as a group.

Our party stayed behind, standing in the rain, while I kept going to find somebody who might be able—and willing—to help us. The visibility was so bad that I could hardly see the road under my feet when I entered this enormous mining area. It was surreal and scary. Machines hummed out of sight, hidden by the fog, and I couldn't tell what direction the sounds were coming from. Finally, the buzz of one of the machines came closer, and then I saw its headlights pierce the fog as it approached me. An enormous mining truck with ten-foot-tall tires pulled up in front of me and stopped when I waved the driver down.

I climbed up the ladder and into the passenger side of the vehicle. The driver was an Indonesian man, and he didn't speak a word to me—didn't even gesture. He just let the vehicle idle. I didn't know what to do, so I took the CB radio, pressed the button to talk, and announced that we were an American climbing team and that we needed a rescue. The voice of an Indonesian man came over the CB radio. Not knowing Indonesian, I couldn't tell what he was saying. I tried to communicate with him to no apparent avail, but still hoped I was getting my point across. I just kept repeating, "We are an American climbing team. An American climbing team …"

We waited in the cab until a land cruiser pulled up alongside the truck. Relieved, I climbed down the ladder. I was expecting the land cruiser to return me to my group and eventually go for help at the mine. I got into the land cruiser and led them back to the group, who were still standing out in the rain by the storage container, only now they were surrounded by several armed security guards.

The head security guard was the only one of them who spoke English. I told him the story of what had happened with the porters, and explained that we needed a rescue to get off the mountain safely. He appeared to be utterly disinterested in anything I was saying. The guards started to leave. Two of the three vehicles drove away. Two of the remaining guards walked over to the storage container and started to unlock it. It began to dawn on me what was about to happen: they intended to lock us in the storage container. I had no idea why. Worse, I had no way to find out. The only guard who spoke English was already gone, and so was our local staff, so we had no way to communicate with the Indonesian guards.

I knew I had to act fast. I motioned for my group to follow me. Several did, but others stayed behind. Meanwhile, the guards were still trying to get the container door open. I suggested that we all sneak over to the land cruiser, which still had the keys in the ignition, and lock ourselves inside. We weren't going to steal the car, just lock ourselves inside so that they would have to call for backup. The hope was that when backup arrived, the guards would abandon their plan to detain us in the storage container.

We snuck over to the vehicle while they were distracted with the storage container, and five of us managed to get into the land cruiser. The security forces came over and tried the doors, but we had locked them. They scowled at us, and motioned us to open the doors, but we refused. We waited for them to call in backup on their radios, which they did.

We sat awkwardly in the car for the next half hour, avoiding eye contact, until another security vehicle pulled up alongside us. The rain continued to pour. Eventually, two more land cruisers pulled up and several guards with semiautomatic weapons and riot gear got out. The head guard, with whom I had spoken earlier, was with them. He came out of the land cruiser carrying a crowbar. Without saying a word, he came up to the vehicle we were in and smashed out the window with me there in the driver's seat. He unlocked the door through the smashed window and pulled me out. He threw me down to the ground at the feet of the other men. I fell in the mud but hoisted myself back up. I put my hands up defensively. Excitement and fear ran through me. I demanded to know who was in charge.

The men ignored me and ordered our whole group into the storage container. My heart sank as they closed the door and the lock clicked into place. I looked around the storage container. We were all crammed together inside very tightly. We had no idea when we would be let out, or even *if* we would be let out.

Thus began one of the strangest ordeals I have ever had to face on a mountain. The hours ticked by slowly. The guards eventually ended up unlocking the container so that we could go outside to attend to necessary body functions, but they put us right back in there immediately after that. We didn't try to escape because we had nowhere to escape to. Sometimes, the guards bullied us by lighting up cigarettes and blowing smoke into our faces. They also tried to talk to us, but we had no way to know what they were saying. I wasn't always sure whether they were being kind or taunting us.

We spent the night in the container. There was very little room to move or lie down. We slept shoulder to shoulder in our sleeping bags, lined up like logs on the floor. The next day the guards brought us a little bit of rice and a small bottle of water for each person, our day's meager rations, which appeared to be the same food ration they gave to the miners.

On the third day, an ambulance came out, and the medics took our blood pressure and other vitals. They recorded this information on a chart. Before leaving, the guards closed the container back up; the guards would come and go throughout the night, visiting us randomly. We spent our third night inside the container, our only possible place of refuge.

By this point, tensions were mounting among our group. Earlier that day, a few Australian miners had stumbled upon us in the storage container. They were shocked, but there wasn't much they could do to help. They left, and came back later with a bag of food for us, mostly just cookies and other junk food. This should have been a blessing, but it ended up causing conflict when people in our group started arguing over how much food each of us had taken from the bag. We were all stressed out, and the bag of junk food just caused unnecessary tension in the group. I wished they had never brought it.

We needed to stay positive. I kept telling myself it would all work out. That was my mantra in the container. *It'll all work out. It'll all work out. It'll all work out.* In the back of my mind, I had doubts about whether this was really true. After a few days like this, you start to lose hope. They could keep us a long time before anyone would notice. We weren't supposed to be back for another week or two, and no one would miss us until then. But to be an effective leader, you have to ignore such doubts. Negativity is contagious, and as leader it was up to me to keep morale high. Leadership means helping people to stay positive, motivated, and cooperative. We were all in this together, and we needed to remember that. We needed to stay strong, work together, and remain patient.

By the fourth day, we were very anxious about what would become of us. We had been stuck in a tiny container for four full days. We were not getting good sleep because the guards kept coming by every couple of hours, day and night, to harass us. I couldn't get any rest because I had to get up and greet them each time.

One time the head guard who spoke English came with them. I spotted him in one of the land cruisers. I went over to the side of his car and bent in to talk to him. I pleaded with him to please let us go and help us get to the airport. I promised we wouldn't cause any problems—we just wanted to go home.

He shook his head impatiently while I talked. Eventually, he turned to me and said, "Go back through the jungle." But I knew we couldn't do that – we were stuck. Our porters were gone, and we had no idea which way to go through the mines.

When I saw him reaching for the shifter to put the vehicle in drive, it was clear to me this was another moment when I had to take action. I went around to the front of the land cruiser and stood directly in front of the vehicle, blocking his way with my body, my hands on the hood of the land cruiser. He tried to nudge me out of the way with the car, but I held my ground as he pushed me slowly. My group, watching this transpire, joined me in blocking the car's path. We boxed him in with our bodies, trapping him just as he had done to us. He revved the engine and tried to nudge us again, but stopped. It was clear he wasn't just going to run us over. So we arrived at a short impasse—we wouldn't move and neither could he.

But it didn't last long. He used his radio to call for backup, and two more cruisers full of security forces showed up and forced us back into the storage container.

We spent another night in the container. Yet again, security guards came in to check on us every couple hours throughout the night. They attempted to intimidate us by waking us up, smoking in the container where we had to sleep, and just coming and going as they pleased without regard for us. In order to try to keep them from coming into the container, I would often try to meet them outside first. The container had become "our" space now, and we didn't want them in it. I would meet the guards outside and try to talk with them, but they continued with the same bullying routine. They would often offer me a cigarette, but rather than actually hand it to me, just blow smoke in my face. They were constantly trying to intimidate us. They stood over us in the container, talking loudly in Indonesian, trying to upset us. They would leave, only to come back an hour or so later and wake us all up again.

No one slept well that night, and by the fifth or sixth day we were utterly exhausted. I struggled to keep morale up and keep the group from turning on one another. We just had to keep it together as a group until an opportunity presented itself, which it did later that day when another car pulled up by the storage container. This one had a single occupant: an American man who was in charge of land-surface engineering at the mine. His name was Alec. He had heard the situation unfolding over the air via the guards' radio communications, and he had finally come to investigate.

He hadn't come earlier for two reasons. First, he didn't have the authority to just come and let us go. Second, there was a major labor crisis at the mine. Thousands of striking workers were blocking the roads to and from the mines, which meant the security forces couldn't have taken us out if they had wanted to. They may well have meant to try to extract money from us for a ride to the airport, but that wasn't even an option due to the demonstrations. The strike had turned into a riot, and two police officers and several miners had been killed. We were stuck in the container because we'd been stuck in the mines. The rioters had made the road impassable by blocking it with large boulders, and it was unsafe to try to drive while the demonstrations were still active.

The American engineer couldn't let us all out of the container for fear of being caught. It was a high-security area, and he didn't have the clearance to let us out and walk us out of the mine. Instead, he allowed me, as the leader of the group, to come up to his office and use the computer. I sent e-mails to embassies and various government agencies to try to get help. I e-mailed my wife, but didn't tell her the specifics because I didn't want to worry her. When I'd finished sending e-mails, he took me back to the storage container.

Over the next few days he came back several times and took other people in our group up to his office to use the computer to try to get a global rescue operation started. We also tried to charter helicopters to come pick us up, but all the helicopters in the area were rented out because of the demonstrations.

The group continued to struggle with internal stress and short tempers while we were held captive in the container. I sent another e-mail to my wife, insisting that everything was okay, but asking her to e-mail me a credit card number with a high credit limit, which she did. I knew it would cost around $10,000 per passenger to pay for a helicopter to fly us all out, if we could even get one, and they would want full payment upfront.

The stalemate continued. We stayed in our container. They would wake us every few hours, occasionally bringing us our rations of rice and water. And every day we snuck up to the computer—putting the engineer at great personal risk—to try to get help. But it was all to no avail. We started to lose track of time. We started to lose hope. But I steeled myself against my despair and resisted negativity. Every day when I came back from the engineer's office, the group asked whom I had e-mailed that day. They wanted big news—but I had nothing for them. There was no rescue underway. No helicopters for rent. There was little hope, and I was afraid it wouldn't turn out okay. Still, I wouldn't let on how scared I was.

Finally, on about the tenth day, our luck changed. Alec, the mine engineer, came and said he had talked to the general manager. "He said to get you guys out of here in the morning on the helicopter."

A complete turn of fortune! After almost two weeks of confinement in a small box, now we were suddenly free to go. We were even being offered aerial transportation. This was a good turn of fortune, but we weren't out of the woods just yet. We still had to get by the security forces, who had so far been very hostile, and onto the helicopter.

That evening, Alec came to drive us out of the mine to his apartment near the helicopter pads. Only six of us would fit in the truck. I stayed behind with three other people, waiting for him to come back for the rest of us later that night. We waited anxiously all night for him to return. The guards continued to check on us periodically. I always met them outside the storage container to prevent them from discovering that half of the group was gone (it's worth it to note that the guards *did* leave our container unlocked, but with nowhere to go and no shelter, we felt forced to stay nearby the container). We were very tense. Alec and the security forces both drove the same white land cruisers. Each time a vehicle pulled up, we had no way of knowing whether it was Alec or the guards.

Alec finally arrived at three o'clock in the morning. He had brought orange vests, safety glasses, and mining helmets to disguise us as miners. We donned all of this accouterment and piled into the back of the vehicle, where we pretended to sleep as we often saw the miners do when they were being transported to and from the mine.

Alec took us through several security checkpoints, at which he was stopped and questioned several times. We drove for more than three hours before we reached the row of little cinder-block houses in the mining village where he lived. The employee housing for the miners looked like an army barracks.

There was a heliport nearby. We could see huge helicopters flying in and out to take miners to and from the airport and mines. We hid in one of the houses until most of the miners had flown out. Finally, once all the miners had been flown in and out, we were loaded onto land cruisers and taken to the heliport. Once there, we boarded a helicopter, and suddenly we were airborne and headed toward the airport. We were the last lift out.

From the helicopter, we could see the jungle below. As we approached the domestic airport in Timika, we saw smoke from burning tires and trees that had been set afire by the striking miners. We landed at the airport, and maybe an hour later we were on a domestic flight to the other side of Indonesia, and then on another plane to Bali, where we had started our trip. It was an incredible change. Hours before we had been held against our will in a storage container, where we had been for almost two weeks, and all of a sudden we are on an airline with stewards coming down the aisle and offering us refreshments. It really put things into perspective for me, and I realized that people in different societies live very different lives, with very different levels of security, respect, and privilege. It gave me an appreciation for my own life and freedoms.

The whole experience also taught me that good leaders must expect the unexpected. The true test of leadership is rising to any challenge. While there are many dangers on the mountain that we come to expect, the bizarre chain of events that led us into that storage container was certainly nothing I could have anticipated or planned for. But I had done my best, refused to give up, and forced myself not to lose hope. I had to persuade myself that it was going to be okay. This was the only way I could maintain hope that we would find a way out.

It really put things into perspective for me, and I realized that people in different societies live very different lives, with very different levels of security, respect, and privilege. It gave me an appreciation for my own life and freedoms.

When the porter came into our camp with a machete or when the armed guards locked us in the container, we could have descended into hysteria and turmoil. But instead I stepped up and accepted a leadership role, and used that role to pull everyone together. Stepping into that leadership role actually inspired me to keep going; by helping others keep hope, I did the same for myself.

I put myself at great risk by being the spokesperson for our group, and by sneaking up into the office building every day, but that was what the situation called for and I knew that someone had to step up and accept that responsibility. We were under great stress from an unexpected situation well beyond the normal stresses of mountain climbing, and the group sorely needed direction and leadership. Someone had to help everyone else hold it all together so that we could work together to do our best to get home safely. So while

> **Sometimes you have to step up|and be a leader, but that doesn't mean you tell people what to do. Great leaders don't delegate, they facilitate. They bring people together.**

our predicament wasn't a typical mountaineering hazard, the goal was the same: to get everyone up and back down the mountain safely. That wasn't going to happen unless someone acted as a facilitator to get the group working together.

Perhaps my biggest takeaway from the trip was the reminder that sometimes you have to step up and be a leader, but that doesn't mean you tell people what to do. Great leaders don't delegate, they facilitate. They bring people together.

CHAPTER FOUR

Snowbird:
The Art and Science of Snow Safety

"The successful warrior is the average man,
with laser-like focus."
—Bruce Lee

For the last twenty-two years, I have been working with the Snow-bird Ski Patrol. As part of Snow Safety, I spent three years as Ski Patrol Director, and now I do avalanche forecasting for Snowbird.

Snowbird is an 11,000-foot mountain in Utah, just outside of Salt Lake City, and the site of Snowbird Ski Resort. Snowbird has some of the best skiing in the country, but it is one of the most avalanche-prone areas, too. My job as an avalanche forecaster for Snow Safety means that I have to battle the very mountain I love on a daily basis each season.

Snowbird has a special place in my heart. It has taught me skills that have helped me in all aspects of my life and career. The experiences I have had on the Snowbird Ski Patrol are the fabric of my life for the last twenty-two years. I was very young when I moved here, only twenty-three years old, and I owe much of my professional development to Snowbird. Some of my greatest mentors in life were here—Peter "Mongo" Schory, Liam Fitzgerald, Randy Trover, and

Jimmy Collinson—and I have formed deep friendships with some of the guests over the years. I also love the mountain itself, which has been both friend and enemy to me.

I work with two other forecasters in the Snow Safety office to carry out avalanche mitigation[8] for the ski resort and other resort workers on the mountain. We work closely with lift operators, the snow cat crew, and the entire mountain operations staff.

Our primary job in snow safety is to monitor the snow conditions and make sure it is safe for people to be on the mountain. We evaluate areas individually to check for instability in the snow. When conditions in the snow are possibly unsafe, we close that area of the resort and check the avalanche potential of the snow. Sometimes we deem it necessary to try to trigger an avalanche by using explosives and military artillery before opening the area back up. Sometimes, we find that the slopes are stable and can be opened up without resorting to mitigation efforts.

Working in snow safety, you develop a special relationship with the snow. You gain an appreciation for how dynamic the snow is. Snow is in a constant state of metamorphism from the moment it falls from the sky. It lies on the surface of the snowpack for a moment, but then changes due to the effects of temperature, pressure, and exposure to sun, wind, and the other elements. Snow is soft and unstable when it first falls, but then it hardens into the snow pack over the course of the season. The snow pack is constantly settling, moving, and changing all across the slopes.

The constant flux in the state of the snowpack is what makes studying snow so interesting. It is also what causes avalanche activity

8 Avalanche prevention and mitigation combines extensive snow pack observation with three major groups of interventions: active (promoting the stabilization and settlement of the snow pack), passive (dams and other deflection devices), and awareness (attempting to modify human behavior that causes avalanches).

on the slopes. The metamorphism process is far from uniform. There can be weak layers[9] buried in the snow pack. As new snow continues to accumulate on top, the weight can cause the weak layer to give. When this happens, the slope fails and you can have a slab avalanche.

Much of my job as an avalanche forecaster involves constantly monitoring snow conditions, issuing opening and closures of areas of the resort, and overall responsibility for snow safety on the mountain. Our team tracks the history of the snow pack across the season, starting with the very first snow of the winter, which usually comes in October (by Thanksgiving we typically have enough snow to open the resort to skiers).

Every year is different. Sometimes the snow comes in and keeps coming, and the snow pack stays stable. Other years the snowpack develops weak layers, which cause avalanches when the pack breaks at the weak layer and the top sloughs off suddenly.

Avalanches tend to occur under certain conditions. You need a slope, usually thirty to forty-five degrees—any steeper and the snow is less likely to accumulate on the slope; less steep, and it won't tend to cascade down. The most sensitive slopes are around thirty-seven degrees, the perfect angle for accumulation and sudden failure of the slope.

You also obviously need snow on the slope. Within that snow, there must be a weak layer at which the pack separates and the top slab slides away suddenly. The weak layer can be anywhere in the snow pack, not just on the surface, which is why we have to track the snowfall over the whole season. Weak layers can have different levels of strength. When the weak layer fails is a function of both the strength of the weak layer and the weight on top of it. When the

9 A weak layer of snow consists of snow that is less cohesive.

strength of the layer is overcome by the weight above it, the layer fails and the slab on top slides down on a bed surface.

Finally, an avalanche needs a trigger. This can be the added weight of freshly fallen snow, or it can be snow deposited on the slope by wind. Heat from the sun can also reduce stability and bring the slope down. Rapid warming produces a wet-slide or loose-snow avalanche, which is different from a slab avalanche caused by a buried weak layer. Lastly, there are manmade triggers such as skiers, snowboarders, snowmobiles, or snowshoes. Avalanches caused by manmade triggers are inherently dangerous because someone is always on the slope when it fails.

> The job of Snow Safety is to detect and mitigate instability in the snowpack so that we can open the resort safely for our guests.

Snowbird is one of the more avalanche-prone resort areas in the United States because of the angle of the slopes that descend into the canyon where the resort sits. This is the perfect angle for skiing and snowboarding … and avalanches. The job of Snow Safety is to detect and mitigate instability in the snowpack so that we can open the resort safely for our guests. This means triggering avalanches preemptively. When doing avalanche mitigation, we first close gates and areas and make sure no one is on the mountain. We have more than a hundred and twenty gates we can open or close so that some areas can be closed off while others are open for the public. In very extreme weather, we may occasionally close the entire resort if necessary. We try to maximize the amount of time that guests can spend on the slopes, but we also want to be sure conditions are safe.

Controlling the snow means getting to know the mountain intimately. We spend much of our time collecting data. We monitor the snow pack from the beginning of the season and record all of the snowfall, wind speeds, wind direction, and other weather data on a continuous basis. We record the density and water weight of the snow and track it throughout the season.

Avalanche forecasting is both a science and an art. You have to know how to collect and interpret data, but you also have to use intuition and follow your gut. Certain quantifiable conditions make avalanches more likely, but interpreting those conditions requires getting out on the mountain and getting a feel for what is happening. This is the art of forecasting—learning what the snow is trying to tell you.

The science part of forecasting requires methodical attention to detail. We start each day the evening before. You have to know the complete history of the snowpack and identify buried weak layers in order to determine how much weight the weak layer can sustain before it fails and causes an avalanche. Before going home, I check overnight forecasts and use them to plan our team's responses for the next day. We take the weather forecast, and based on what we had open for the day (sometimes if a section of the mountain was open all day, it's easier to just keep it open rather than opening a section that had just been closed—we have to see how the weather changed throughout the day, and then make the decision on opening vs reopening), we determine what our course of action will be the following day. Before going home, I speak with the snow cat operators who will be on the mountain overnight. We make closures to areas based on the weather forecast so that we are ready for the morning.

The next morning, I'm up at four o'clock and at the office well before sunrise. I check the new forecasts and go to the snow study plot to gather information from our snow gauges. We take the snowfall measurements at the base and collect data from different mountain locations. We calculate the depth of the snowfall and the weight of the snow, its density, its water content, and so on. We look at wind direction and wind speeds and try to calculate where snow might have been transported. We check cameras and forecasts. We run reports. We pull data from the weather stations hourly reports. We comb the data. We look at current temperatures at the peak and tram base[10] and track how they changed overnight.

In addition to checking the weather stations, I check different snow stakes[11] and storm stakes[12] to monitor snowfall directly. This is an important part of the process. Really getting my hands in the snow and feeling it helps me make more intuitive decisions. You get a sixth sense about these things, and for me at least, it's very tactile. I have to be present on the mountain and in the snow.

This is one of the parts I like best—gearing up and putting on my skis and going out into the crisp morning air. There's a calm in those early morning hours when no one is on the mountain yet, and it's still dark out and everything is quiet. It empties you out inside. You have to have complete focus. You can't be susceptible to distractions.

Once we are done combing through the data, I reconvene with my partners and team up on Hidden Peak, where the ski patrol headquarters are, at 11,000 feet. We revise the day's plan and start delegating tasks. Then it's time to start active mitigation efforts. At

---

10 The tram base is what's at the bottom of the mountain.
11 Snow stakes are the boards that we clear and then collect the new fallen snow so we can measure the new snow and collect a sample for data; depth, weight and water content of the new fallen snow. We have 3 snow stakes; One interval stake (dumped every 12 hours; one 24 hour stake dumped each morning; one storm stake that runs from the time it starts snowing until it stops snowing.
12 Storm stakes are run throughout the entire storm.

this point, we are actively hunting down avalanches to set them off preemptively. Regardless of whether we find snow instability issues or not, we make our observations and move on to the next slope. Bringing loose slopes down is a kind of precise demolition. Watching the snow cascade down the mountain, falling where and when we want it to, can be exhilarating and rewarding. You are both controlling and working with nature at the same time, working with and against the mountain.

We test the stability of slopes we suspect may be unstable by trying to bring them down. We shoot cannons high above these areas and then the ski patrol runs avalanche control routes. The cannons are used in areas that are difficult to get to on skis. Once we shoot the cannons, we can come in below those areas and ski through on our predefined control routes. Each of the patrol teams on these routes checks multiple starting zones and determines whether to ski cut[13] or shoot the slope to test its stability with explosives.

They move carefully and progress slowly across the slopes, moving one at a time through danger zones to the next island of safety.[14] Safety is a primary concern. We go in teams so that we only expose one person to hazard at a time. We all are in constant radio contact with Hidden Peak dispatch and adjacent patrol routes. We all wear transceivers and carry shovels, probes, and rescue gear in our patrol packs.

Deciding whether to detonate or try a ski test to see if anything sloughs off requires a deep understanding of the mountain and the snow. I have to really trust my crew here, both for their safety and everyone else's—and I do trust them. We are a team. We rely on one another. We trust one another. We work together.

---

13 A ski cut is a technique where we ski across the top of an avalanche starting zone and try to start a small slide mainly the new snow.
14 An island of safety is an area where you are less exposed to the hazard of an avalanche, e.g., under cliff bands, below trees, or on a ridge line..

Communication is important, as it is with any endeavor in which precision counts and stakes are high—and both of these things are certainly true with snow safety and avalanche control. We have to communicate effectively to make sure everything goes safely and according to plan. Once we send people out on routes, we stay in contact by radio and track them through the mountain dispatch. We check in with every single person every fifteen minutes. Things can change quickly on the mountain, and we need to know where each team is at all times.

We also have to communicate with people outside Snow Safety. We do most avalanche mitigation early in the morning, before opening the resort to the public, but we are not the only workers on the mountain. We have to ensure that the areas we are shooting are clear of snow cat drivers, plow drivers, and all mountain operations employees. We close the mountain so there are no people wandering around who would interfere with our work. This requires a massive communication effort involving the snow safety team, ski patrol, the lift operators, and the leaders of any other work crews on the mountains—and it must continue every single day and night of the season. The snow cats groom the snow before the resort opens, and we have to make sure they are off the slopes when we are shooting. Snow makers work overnight too, so we have to know if they are still out on the slopes. We also make overnight forecasts for them so they know which slopes aren't safe, which ones need snow made, and so forth. Our work is ongoing—the job basically doesn't end until the season does.

Part of good communication is trust. If you don't have trust, you will not be able to delegate tasks, which means you won't be an effective leader and you won't get a full picture that you can … well, trust. There is no way you can micromanage everything on the mountain yourself. You have to trust your team to report things accurately and make the right calls on their own. This is important as a forecaster, because I can't be everywhere at once. So I have to trust my men with their "skis in the snow" to report accurately and fully, and I have to accept their input into my decisions as if it were my own. They have to earn that trust, but once they do, I have to grant it and stick to it, and not second-guess them unduly.

Communication with my team isn't a one-way street. Yes, I have to be able to communicate big picture objectives to them, but I rely on them for the details. Communication helps make sure we all have the whole picture. This is absolutely necessary. None of us work every day, but we still have to know what has been happening on the mountain for the past week in order to forecast avalanche danger. And it is the guys out on skis who know—for sure—what is happening on any particular route at any particular moment. I have to listen to them carefully and trust what they are saying in order to synthesize everything. This allows me to maintain an overall picture of what we are doing.

We try to make the slopes safe so we can open for business by 9:00 a.m. and guests can enjoy them, but it isn't always possible. Every day is different. Some days we can't open the whole mountain, especially after a big snow or if it is still actively snowing. We open the slopes in segments, usually starting with those closest to the tram. Gad Valley, Peruvian Gulch, Mineral Basin, Gad II, Little Cloud, Baldy … there are more than 120 avalanche flip-signs (open/closed gates) to indicate where people can and can't ski.

The goal here is to open and keep open as many slopes as possible, but without letting people onto slopes that might fail. We close areas in segments as needed, and the more it snows, the more segments it may become necessary to close down. On very heavy snow days, we may have to close an area for the entire day, or even multiple days during a storm. Other days, the weather will be good and you can open up the whole mountain "wall to wall," as we say.

When the danger for inbound avalanches—those that will come down the canyon and threaten the resort—is high, we put everything on lockdown. We give the signal and everyone is ordered indoors and all the buildings are locked and chained, even private residences. This is referred to as "interlodge," meaning that everyone must stay indoors while we do avalanche control work above the Snowbird Village and on the highway. This is important because, while most experienced skiers understand the danger, some people just don't realize how dangerous avalanches are. It's not a big fluffy cloud coming down the mountain. It is a pack of snow that can move up to a hundred miles per hour, taking out everything in its path. I have seen avalanches take out the entire parking lot, destroying dozens of vehicles. I have seen avalanches take out structures (Snowbird's buildings are concrete-reinforced and designed to withstand the impact of an avalanche). I have also seen avalanches hit the resort buildings and the parking lot, and take out forests of hundred-year-old trees.

I don't want to make it sound like Snowbird is a deathtrap—it's not. Thousands of people visit each year and go home safely. But that is because of the diligent work of ski patrol and the snow safety crew. We don't let ourselves forget that; even though the resort is all about fun on the snow most of the time, we also bear an immense responsibility. As the people in charge of safety, we have to remember that people's lives are on the lines when we make a forecast, when we decide to open the resort, or when we decide whether to shoot a slope or not. It is heady stuff. Great responsibility comes with each decision we make every day.

We have to be able to accept this responsibility if we are going to do the job. We like to keep the slopes open as much as possible (as I like to say, we provide "powder to the people!"), but sometimes mistakes happen. This is the inevitable consequence of quantifying risk—the smallest calculated risks occasionally lead to outcomes you don't want. We have had inbound avalanches hit the resort and come down on the slopes without warning. We will get a call from the ski patrol that they have found some avalanche debris, and all of the sudden we switch into "hasty search rescue mode." We look quickly for visual clues, transceiver signals, and Recco reflectors. We bring out the rescue dogs and probe the snow. This is the initial hasty search to find any potential victims who might be buried in the snow. Usually everyone is okay, but sometimes not.

A few of years ago an inbound avalanche cost a twenty-three-year-old girl her life. We conducted a hasty search and rescue effort in the areas where numerous had been skiing and snowboarding, and we found one victim under the snow. I will never forget that day—the decisions and the rescue effort. You live with that kind of accident every day for the rest of your life. I personally thought about that girl every day for a long time, and I still think of her regularly. That kind of tragedy can really make you second-guess yourself. But you have to remember that this is *precisely* what you are there to avoid, and you do all you can to prevent something like that from ever happening again. You can never allow yourself to be complacent.

This is the kind of responsibility that high-stakes decision makers have to accept if they want to *be* decision-makers. Maybe you don't have lives on the line in your job, but the stakes are still high if you are a decision-maker in any field. People's careers are on the line, profits, livelihoods. I feel this now in my current role as CEO of a new small business and nonprofit. If you can't own up to the responsibility of your decisions, you shouldn't be making decisions in the first place.

By saying that, I don't mean to be condescending—I simply mean that everyone in a leadership role needs to step up and take responsibility for their decisions. That's true in avalanche forecasting and it's true in every other field as well, whether the stakes are high or low.

This doesn't mean you have to be perfect. Mistakes happen. You get caught off guard sometimes. There is no way to know with 100 percent certainty when an avalanche will be triggered. My mentor at Snowbird, Mongo, used to tell me that the only thing we know for sure is that, "When it snows, we get avalanches." A dozen skiers can go over a slope no problem, and then one more goes and the slope fails.

This is where the art of forecasting comes in. The science of forecasting involves reading and interpreting the data, but decisions must often be made from the gut. The science helps you quantify the risk, but it won't tell you if there is going to be an avalanche or not. To do that, you have to develop a feel for the mountain and the snow. You have to take in all the details, but focus on the big picture.

In the end, you have to trust your intuition. All the times I made mistakes were times when I had considered closing an area of the resort, but didn't trust my own intuition. I "thought" myself out of doing what I knew, deep down inside, was the right thing to do.

The longer you do something, the more you hone your craft, the better you get at it. As an avalanche forecaster, it is so important to know how the snow feels under your skis, how fresh snow reacts, and how it is different every time it snows. Just being in the snow tells you something about it, if you learn to listen. Eventually you develop an intuition and start making decisions with confidence—that is the mark of someone who understands the art of forecasting.

I love to be out there on the slopes and in the snow. You get a sense for what you see, how the snow is falling, and how it sloughs off trees. It helps you interpret the data and put it into real-world terms. The science of forecasting helps you figure out the probabilities of certain outcomes, but it doesn't tell you the consequence of each action. That is something you have to learn and internalize by practicing your trade.

> The science of forecasting helps you figure out the probabilities of certain outcomes, but it doesn't tell you the consequence of each action. That is something you have to learn and internalize by practicing your trade.

You have to practice forecasting to become good at it. It requires practice, dedication, and mindfulness. It is, in some ways, similar to the scientific method. You have to form a hypothesis based on what you think you will see in the snow, make observations, and then reflect on your hypothesis and see if you were right, wrong, or even close. Then you make the most accurate forecast you can. The more you do this, the better at it you get. Reflecting on your decisions and evaluating them makes you a better forecaster.

People often think of me as an adventurous person who ignores risk, but the truth is that leading an adventurous life has actually made me more aware of risk. If I have to decide whether or not to cross a danger zone on a ski cut, I am going to be very aware of exactly how doing so might trigger an avalanche, and whether it would put me at risk of getting caught in the avalanche and sent down into the rocks and trees, or buried. There is a certain amount of acceptable risk in this kind of work, but making sure that risk is acceptable means understanding the risk and being carefully attuned to it.

More than even my own safety, I worry about the safety of others. I think about the resort guests, my ski patrol guys on the slopes, and other people working at the resort. Once we give the okay to open the slopes, anyone can go out on them. I take this very seriously, and always try to err on the side of safety when making decisions. If an area has to be shut down, I am ready to shut it down.

That said, you also have to consider the consequences of shutting the resort down. My job would be a lot easier, and no one would ever get hurt, if we kept the slopes shut down all the time, but that's not what the guests want or what they are paying me to do. They pay us to close down parts of the resort only when the conditions are unsafe. This is a hard balance to strike, and it sometimes requires us to make tough choices.

The choices may be tough, but they have to be made. I have found that, if you have carefully weighed your options and the consequences of your actions, and if you are ready to take responsibility for those consequences, you can make decisions with confidence and hold your head high. That's really all you can do.

You have to make choices that you can live with. This means paying attention, not getting complacent, and carefully considering the consequences of your decisions. Do this, and you can make choices that you can stand behind, no matter the eventual outcome. Even if something goes wrong, you will know you did your best and based your decision on sound decision-making practices.

When making such weighty decisions, it is natural to be scared. It is okay to be scared, and you have to avoid overconfidence, but you also have to be ready to act. This means that you need to embrace fear and still be able to proceed. Everyone doubts themselves sometimes—this is a sign of critical thinking and self-awareness—but at the end of the day you need to be able to be confident in your decisions if you are going to make them.

How do you tell confidence from overconfidence? By how well you back up your decisions. Your decisions should always be backed up by the data you have collected, wisdom gleaned from past experiences, trust in your team, and ultimately, trust in yourself. There may always be fear of negative consequences, but you must proceed with confidence. If you put effort into collecting information and weighing the consequences, you will be able to make your decision and live with the consequences, no matter what.

CHAPTER FIVE

Wasatch Backcountry Rescue:
The Best Rescue Is the One That Need Never Occur

"A winner is one who accepts his failure and mistakes, picks up the pieces, and continues striving to reach his goals."
—Dexter Yager

The Wasatch Backcountry Rescue (WBR) group was established in 1977 after a backcountry avalanche tragedy in Little Cottonwood Canyon, Utah. WBR is a group of highly trained professional rescuers from the nine Utah ski resorts and seven other professional organizations, including AirMed International, Life Flight Network, the Utah Department of Transportation, the United States Forest Service, and the Wasatch Powderbird Guides. WBR's professional rescuers respond outside the boundaries of the ski areas in order to assist five county sheriff agencies with backcountry avalanche and mountain rescue.

> Snow safety and rescue are two sides of the same coin.

Rescue is exciting and rewarding work. It is also frequently necessary in the mountains. While working in snow safety at Snowbird, I began to realize that, while snow safety focuses on avoiding accidents and mistakes, sometimes they happen anyway. When something does go wrong, that is when the rescuers come in. Snow safety and rescue are two sides of the same coin.

I began working with WBR early in my patrol career. I started as rescuer and dog handler. Over time I moved up, first to WBR rescue dog coordinator and eventually to president of the organization, but I remained a rescuer and dog handler the entire time. When I became president in 1999, WBR was a small organization. We didn't even have a logo, and certainly no website. We had limited funds to work with, but we didn't let this deter us from getting the job done right.

It was an honor to serve as president of the Wasatch Backcountry Rescue for over a decade. In that time, I did my best to grow and refine the program. I raised hundreds of thousands of dollars, money that allowed us to grow the organization. During my tenure as president, we introduced new technologies, such as numerous automated transceiver-training centers where the public could practice rescue-beacon skills[15]. We implemented the first helicopter-based transceiver system, the Long Range Receiver (LRR)[16], the first of its kind to be utilized in the United States. I trained numerous pilots and flight crews in the use of this system, and WBR now has eight LRR-equipped aircrafts in the Salt Lake City area. I also helped train pilots from the Washington State National Guard, and this

---

15 Avalanche beacon (also known as avalance transceivers) are a class of active radio transceivers specialized for the purpose of finding people buried under snow. The transceiver emits a low-power pulsed beacon signal during the trip. If the person holding the transceiver is safe from an avalanche (for example), they may switch the transceiver from transmit into receive mode, allowing them to use their device to search for signals coming from other skiers' transmitter beacons who may be trapped, or nearby. These are most importantly used to find someone buried under the snow.

16 The LRR is a device we use from the helicopter to find someone wearing and transceiver; this device differs from the Avalance Beacon, because we are searching from the helicopter as opposed to searching from the ground.

program has now expanded beyond Utah, into Washington State and Colorado.

WBR also hosted numerous avalanche rescue dog schools with professional rescue teams from all over the western United States and Canada. We worked hard on testing and training consistency. As a result, we now have numerous excellent dog teams. We also set up educational programs to teach the public about better decision-making in the backcountry. In 2007 WBR was inducted into the International Commission of Alpine Rescue (ICAR) as a United States representative and member, joining a network of thirty-eight countries from around the world.

Working with the Wasatch Backcountry Rescue, I gained a lifelong respect for the mountains. When you love being in the mountains as much as I do and have seen as much as I have, you never forget that for all the beauty and adventure they offer, the mountains can be dangerous. They are places of recreation, but they can turn on you in a minute if the weather or slope conditions become active.

Most people who visit the mountains will never see what can go wrong firsthand, but working backcountry rescue, you often witness tragedies up close. Seeing the outcome of an accident changes the

The mountain always decides, and it is up to us to react on her terms.

way you approach the mountains. You become more aware of your surroundings and the consequences of your decisions. You strive to always be observant of your surroundings. You never go out unprepared. You don't let yourself become complacent. You keep your guard up. You make plans, but you learn to keep them flexible. The mountains deserve respect. The mountain always decides, and it is up to us to react on her terms. You need to react to the environment, as it changes you need to adapt to it. Rescue work is a harrowing reminder of the potential consequences when you make a mistake, ignore risks, or lapse in your respect for the mountains.

It is often family that first alerts us to the need for a rescue. Typically, we get a call at night when someone hasn't returned from the backcountry or the slopes. A classic case is that of Bruce Quint and Mel Dennis, two men who went missing while snowshoeing in the backcountry in Big Cottonwood Canyon in 2004. When they didn't come home at the end of the day, their significant others drove up the canyon. The car the men had taken was parked at the trailhead, but they were nowhere to be found. The family members then phoned the police, who phoned us to request a rescue.

That night we went out with the helicopters to conduct an aerial search. We didn't find them. It was far too dangerous to go in on the ground and conduct a night search. The following morning, we spotted their snowshoe tracks from the air. We saw two sets of tracks side by side, and then one set of tracks where they were following each other in the deep snow. The tracks went into the slide debris, but didn't come out the other side, which told us that they were in the slide debris.

The two men had triggered a sympathetic avalanche[17] while hiking a trail on the valley floor. They didn't trigger it from the starting zone, but their movements caused the weak snowpack to come down on top of them. This was a worst-case scenario because it resulted in them being on the very bottom of the deposition area[18] when the snow came down. They probably looked up and saw it rushing down on them, but there was nowhere to go.

17 A sympathetic avalanche is an avalanche that releases in direct response to a neighboring avalanche or a remote trigger.
18 This is the pile of snow / the avalanche debris.

Before we could go down and do a search, we had to make sure the area was safe. We started by marking the corners of the debris with the GPS from the helicopter, in case another big slide came down during the search, making the search area even larger. In such an event, we would still know where the original slide had occurred. Next we did a helicopter bombing mission with explosives to bring down any potential avalanches in the area, making the area safe for the rescuers to go in. When we start a search like this, our first priority is to ensure the safety of the rescuers. Only then are we able to help. Once we had made the area safe, we started the search.

There are two stages to a snow rescue search. The first is what we call the hasty search. At this stage, you are still hoping for a live recovery. You have to move fast, and focus on the basics of avalanche rescue. This has to be so ingrained that you do it on autopilot. First, we make sure the area is safe, and that another avalanche won't bury our search party (this is why we did the bombing from the helicopter). We also post an avalanche guard to watch for secondary avalanches and alert the team to retreat to cover by a predetermined route if it becomes necessary.

Once safety is established, we start looking for the victims. We first check for a transceiver signal to see if the victim is wearing one. If they are, locating them is much easier. If there is no transceiver signal, we use a Recco detector, which will alert to the presence of Recco reflectors under the snow.[19] These reflectors are now commonly sewn into skiing gear by manufacturers.

In this case, there was no transceiver or Recco signal. Next we

---

19 The Recco system consists of two parts: a reflector integrated into clothing, boots, and body protection worn by skiers; and a detector used by rescue teams. The detector sends out a signal that bounces back if it hits a reflector. The returned signal is translated into an audio tone whose volume is proportional to the returned signal, enabling a trained operator to find the buried reflector.

performed a quick visual search of the slide path. Sometimes you will see a hand, a ski, or a boot or something sticking out of the snow. We also had searchers probe the most likely areas as determined by the way the snow had deposited. We could see where the men's footprints disappeared, which enabled us to deduce where the slide might have taken them. Unfortunately, since they were in the deposition area, they were probably very deep.

While some rescuers were performing the tasks described above, others worked the search dogs. The dogs are trained to detect human scent, which percolates to the top of the snowpack. Search dogs play a crucial role, and there is still no better technology for finding a body in the snowpack than a dog's nose. My dog, Midas, has since passed away, but he was an indispensable partner. Former President Jimmy Carter once told me, when we were doing rescue drills for the Carter Foundation, that he could see I was really proud of my dog. I am proud of all the rescue dogs, and we couldn't have done this job without them. Dogs usually offer the best chance to find someone who isn't wearing a transceiver or a Recco reflector. If the dog alerts on an area, we then do a quick probe search to find the body. If we strike the victim, we start digging.

We soon found Mel Dennis buried under five feet of snow, but we couldn't find Bruce Quint. We had multiple dogs and patrollers shoulder to shoulder, probing down into the snow, but we still couldn't locate him. We returned to the staging area where the victim's family was with the sheriff's command post. The victim's wife was in tears, and I made a promise to her: "We're going to find him tomorrow."

I regretted those words even as they came out of my mouth. Sometimes we didn't find bodies until the snowpack melted in the spring. There was no guarantee that we would find him tomorrow, or even at all. I stayed up all night tossing and turning, regretting what I had said, worried we wouldn't recover him and that I had given her false hope.

The next day, we started the secondary search, which is the search for the body. The hasty search is about speed and maximizing the chance of a live recovery, but the ongoing search is about finding the body to bring closure to the case. We still hope for a live recovery, but the longer the victim is under the snow, the less likely that is. You know this, but you still hope. At this point, however, there was no way Bruce was still alive.[20]

During the secondary search, you take your time and search methodically. Time is no longer of the essence, although finding the body quickly helps the family achieve closure. In the search for Bruce, I acted as accident site commander. I managed communications and logistics, determined the most likely spots to look, and helped organize the effort to probe the entire slide area.

Meanwhile, my partner, Kevin Meadows, worked the dog, Midas, who eventually alerted to the victim's scent. He had been too far down for the scent to percolate to the top of the snowpack the night before, but now it had had time to make its way to the surface. We were able to find the body with the probe, and we started digging through ten feet of avalanche debris that was packed hard like concrete. Finally, we found Bruce.

I was relieved to be able to tell his wife we had found her husband, but it was hard for me to keep it together in front of the family. They invited me to the funeral, which I politely declined. This happens a lot. As much as I want to support people, we don't know the victims, and there are so many tragedies. You never really get numb

---

20 Even if you survive the impact of the slide, after fifteen minutes buried under the snow your survival chances drop to 30 percent, and they continue to drop rapidly from there as time passes.

to them, and so you have to maintain a certain distance in order to do the job.

This part of the job gets really hard. The sad truth about avalanche rescues is that they rarely end well. You always aim for live recovery, but they are exceedingly rare. I have only ever had one live recovery in an avalanche situation, and the circumstances surrounding it were extraordinary. I was working at Snowbird when a call came over the radio from Liam Fitzgerald, the director of the Utah Department of Transportation's avalanche program. He had been on the ridge across the canyon from Snowbird, out checking conditions above the highway, when he saw a skier traveling up a skin track[21]. Suddenly, the slope failed on the skier. Liam watched as the skier was caught in the slide and engulfed in snow.

For a man swept away in an avalanche, he was very lucky. Not only did Liam see the accident, there also happened to be a helicopter already near Snowbird. The Wasatch Powderbird Guides were flying close to the area when the call came in, and they diverted to Hidden Peak to pick Midas and me up so we could participate in the rescue. I was trying to think live recovery, but I was already steeling myself against the likelihood of another dead avalanche victim.

Another stroke of luck: a nearby ski party[22] had also seen the accident and come to the man's rescue. By the time we got there, the ski party had already picked up the victim's transceiver signal and had started to probe for him. I told Midas to stay, and my partner, Sam Davis, and I started digging. The man was down about five feet deep. He was already going grey due to asphyxiation when we

---

21 A skin track is the route that you set as you ascend when you are using climbing skins on your skis. This route is often set and then others can follow it. It is the path in the snow when you break trail.

22 A ski party is just as it sounds – a group of people out for a day of back country skiing. Since they are in the backcountry they are (usually) equipped with avalanche rescue gear – transceivers, shovels, and probe so they are ready to do a rescue if one of their friends are caught and buried.

uncovered his head.[23] His eyes were open, but he was unresponsive. Sam cleared out his airway, and suddenly the man's legs started to move and he began to come around. He was moaning, asking what had happened and how deeply he'd been buried. He was talking slowly. I asked him for an emergency contact, in case he blacked out again, and he told me his wife's name: "Patricia. Patricia Hansen." He also gave us her phone number.

At about this time, the air ambulance arrived. We loaded him onto a stretcher and got him into the helicopter, and they rushed him to a hospital. He ended up living, and a few days later he called to thank us. I never heard from him again, but he stuck with me because he was my first—and so far only—live recovery from an avalanche. Usually we find the bodies of any victims and then have to go straight back to work, but that day we finally pulled someone out of the snow alive!

This is why you always push for the live rescue despite the odds. You move fast, communicate well, focus on the basics, and work methodically but quickly on the off chance that the victim is still alive. Eventually, it pays off. Saving that one man's life made all those failed attempts worthwhile. It also gave me hope to continue trying to save others.

Unfortunately, as I have already indicated, this is exceedingly rare. By the time professionals arrive on the scene, the chances of survival have usually gone way down. Your best chance of surviving an avalanche is for someone who is there with you to dig you out. This man was lucky that the ski party had seen him, and still he almost hadn't made it. If you are wearing a transceiver and someone

---

23 Two thirds of avalanche victims who survive the impact of being buried die of asphyxiation. If the victim has protected their airway or can clear it, then they can usually breathe. While they remain trapped, however, either the surrounding air will be exhausted or the victim's respiration will condense and freeze slowly around their face, forming an ice mask that traps their exhaled carbon dioxide and suffocates them.

with you digs you out in five or ten minutes, you will probably live. After fifteen minutes, however, your chances of survival drop to 30 percent and fall off a cliff shortly after that. Occasionally someone will live for an hour or more if they end up buried with an air pocket around their head, but this is rare. Few people walk away from an avalanche if they are buried.[24]

In the late nineties, we had a backcountry avalanche that buried two teenagers under a few feet of snow. They were blue and unresponsive when we dug them up. We gave them CPR, but we were unsuccessful and they could not be revived. I knew then that educating the public was the only answer. We had to teach people to avoid accidents. This just goes to show: snow safety and mountain rescue go hand in hand. Preventing an accident is always preferable to attempting a rescue. At WBR, we know that we can't usually save you by digging you out of the snow.

> Preventing an accident is always preferable to attempting a rescue.

Doing good rescue work is important, but few people survive avalanches. My best chance of saving someone's life as a rescuer is to teach them how to avoid accidents in the first place, and what to do in the event of an accident.

Since then, I have incorporated safety into everything I do in the mountains. Whenever I talk to someone on the mountain, I try to educate them about mountain safety. Shortly after that incident, I launched a free one-hour class on avalanche transceiver skills, coupled with a six-hour field course. The following week, we did a six-hour field course in the basics of avalanche awareness. We covered snow pack evaluation, how to move safely so that the whole

---

24 Each year avalanches kill more than 150 people worldwide.

party doesn't get buried, safety gear, snow pack evaluation, the signs of instability, safe travel, and self-rescue.

Prevention is all about being aware of your surroundings and making the right decisions about safety. You need to come prepared with a partner. You both need to be wearing transceivers and know how to use them. You need a shovel and a probe at the minimum—the transceiver leads to the probe, the probe leads to the shovel, and the shovel leads to your partner. You need all three for a speedy recovery. Plus, you must have the knowhow to use these tools quickly in that key moment when your partner is first buried.

You have to be able to recognize and avoid hazardous conditions. Sometimes this means going up a different slope. Sometimes, when conditions are bad, it means getting off the mountain. Bruce and Mel, the two snowshoers caught in the avalanche that I mentioned earlier, had been out on the mountains on a high-hazard day. There were four fatalities in Utah that week alone. I myself had been in an avalanche accident while doing snow safety work at Snowbird the very day before! Had the two men looked at the avalanche bulletin, they might have stayed out of the canyon. Either they didn't know any better, or they chose to ignore the signs of instability on the slopes. They shouldn't have been out there at all that day.

There are a lot of tools out there. There are classes like the ones we offer, and there are avalanche forecasts available to you, like the ones we do for Snowbird Snow Safety. For example, the Utah Avalanche Center puts out a great daily bulletin on the avalanche forecast.

The most important thing is simply to respect the mountain. For mountain activities to be safe—for any activity to be safe—you have to practice safety protocols. Don't get overconfident. Respect the mountain. The mountain decides. What you have to decide is how to react to her. Sometimes that means being slow and careful. Other times, it means packing up and going home to come back another day.

In the end, your safety is up to you. I am proud to have saved several lives while working with WBR, but I am more proud of the prevention and education programs I helped to put in place. At the end of the day, only you can keep yourself safe in the mountains.

Dean on the Summit of Mt. Everest

View of Mt. Everest from Kala Patthar

Our team on Mt. Everest

The Western Khum on Mt. Everest

Mt. Everest Camp III, the Lhotse Face, 24,500'

Back down through the ice fall on Mt. Everest (Pumori in background)

Crossing through the Khumbu icefall, Mt. Everest

Everest Base Camp with the Khumbu Ice Fall looming in the background

Tyrolean traverse, Carstensz Pyramid

The container with Carstensz Pyramid in the background

The natives on our way to Carstensz Pyramid

Snowbird Ski Patrol shooting the Willows gun (105 mm recoilless rifle) above the highway in Little Cottonwood Canyon to open the highway and Snowbird village during high avalanche hazard (photo by Andrew Miller)

Snowbird Ski Patrol heading out to run avalanche control routes (photo by John Collins)

Snowbird Avalanche Control Work (photo by John Collins)

Snowbird Ski Patrol

President Jimmy Carter
with Dean and Midas
Snowbird

WBR Dean and Midas searching a large slide, Summit County, Utah

Guiding on Kilimanjaro (photo by Jay Dash)

Guiding on Kilimanjaro (photo by Jay Dash)

Shira Camp on Kilimanjaro (12,500')

Priscilla and Art Ulene summit Kilimanjaro, Uhuru Peak 19,340'

Alison above the clouds, Ecuador, Cotopaxi

Ecuador, Cotopaxi (19,347')

A look at the upper mountain from Camp 1, Tibet, Cho Oyu

Himalayan Children's Foundation, Nepal

Dean with Pasang's family in Nepal, Human Outreach Project (HOP)

Humble beginnings at the HOP Kilimanjaro Kids Community (HOP KKC), construction of the first building in Tanzania

Dean helping wash
hands at the HOP KKC

Nema and Dean at the HOP KKC

Ready to fly in and get dropped off on the Kahiltna glacier, Alaska

Mt. Mckinley, Alaska (Denali) 20,237'

CHAPTER SIX

Kilimanjaro:
The True Essence of Guiding

"Life is not measured by the number of breaths we take,
but by the moments that take our breath away."
—Maya Angelou

Kilimanjaro is a dormant volcano that stands alone on the African plains. Kilimanjaro is the tallest mountain in Africa, making it one of the Seven Summits.[25] It is also the largest freestanding mountain in the entire world, which makes its high altitudes particularly awe-inspiring when seen in person. The mountain is often partially obscured by cloud cover, but when the skies clear, Kilimanjaro is an impressive sight. It rises steeply and gently from the African plains to a glacier-capped crater.

As a professional guide, I have climbed Kilimanjaro more than thirty-five times with people and trekkers from all walks of life. I've taken hundreds of people to the summit and back down again. Kilimanjaro is very popular with new climbers and trekkers because, despite its high altitude of 19,341 feet, it is a relatively nontechnical

---

25 The Seven Summits are the highest mountains of each of the seven continents. It is considered a mountaineering challenge to summit all of them. The first person to do so was Richard Bass, on April 30, 1985.

climb. You don't need crampons, ice axes, helmets, ropes, or any other specialized gear or training. There are few other places in the world where you can approach 20,000 feet without technical climbing skills.

For this reason, Kilimanjaro is often underestimated by would-be climbers. For the average person with little climbing experience, trekking on Kilimanjaro presents a substantial—but generally suitable—challenge. But Kilimanjaro should not be underestimated. Nontechnical does not mean easy. There is nothing easy or routine about going up past 19,000 feet. Such altitudes invariably mean that summiting will require a climber to contend with extreme cold and low oxygen (half that of sea level). I have guided many, many people up Kilimanjaro, and many of them have told me it was the hardest thing they've ever done in their lives.

> I have guided many, many people up Kilimanjaro, and many of them have told me it was the hardest thing they've ever done in their lives.

This doesn't mean that Kilimanjaro cannot be attempted by anyone in good health—it can be. Nearly all of my guests reach the summit. Some think they can't, but they do. They just need the proper motivation and guidance, which is where I come in.

I tell people considering climbing Kilimanjaro that while it's not easy, it is exciting, and it is within the reach of most people. The climb is amazing, the views breathtaking, and the sense of achievement substantial. Summiting Kilimanjaro and getting back down again is a huge accomplishment, and dismissing the climb as easy does an injustice not only to the mountain, but also to the accomplishments of those who have successfully climbed it.

Kilimanjaro is one of my favorite places to guide. Whenever I take a group there (or anywhere, for that matter), I tell them that we all have the same goal. While each person may be there for different reasons, we all have the same collective aspiration. Some are there because they have been dreaming of Kilimanjaro for years. Others want to accomplish something to share with friends. Some are simply there in support of a spouse who wanted to go. Whatever their reasons for being on the mountain, they all have the same goal: to summit the mountain and get back down safely. My goal is to help get them—all of them—to the top and back down safely. This means that we will all accomplish our goals together. They may not always understand why I am asking them to do something, but it is always in service of this goal.

I also tell them that, while I know they can accomplish this goal, it will not be easy. It may sometimes be uncomfortable. I will sometimes push them to do difficult things. I have learned in the mountains that success often times means finding some comfort in being uncomfortable. You have to expect—and accept—a certain level of discomfort when doing something like climbing Kilimanjaro.

The above is, in short, the true essence of guiding. Good guiding involves pushing people beyond what they think they can do, but not beyond what they are capable of doing. Many people don't recognize the full extent of their abilities. But with proper encouragement, you can motivate people to go outside their comfort zones and all the way to the limit of their potential. They can almost always push themselves further, even when they think they have to quit. This is why they need a good guide—someone to cheer them on and remind them that they can do this.

On Kilimanjaro, the hardest part is the summit day. This is when you spend the most time at high altitudes. The lack of oxygen makes every step harder. When people aren't accustomed to the effects of high altitude, they sometimes think they cannot make it when really, they can. This is where I come in as a guide. Normally, I assess the situation to determine whether they really can continue forward—in most cases, they just need a little encouragement. I tell them to stop and take a rest, and then we will continue. We accomplish a series of mini goals, knowing that achieving our ultimate goal will be the end result.

Of course, as a guide I have to be aware when someone really is at their limit. Good guiding involves pushing people all the way to the edge of their comfort zone, but not beyond the point of what they are capable of doing. You have to go right up to that edge without crossing over it. As a guide on Kilimanjaro, the last thing I want is to take someone up over 19,000 feet only for them to be unable to get down safely and have to be rescued off the mountain. This has never been a problem on a World Wide Trekking trip because I am careful to observe my guests' limits and encourage them to pull back if necessary. Generally, this is not a problem. In more than thirty-five trips to Kilimanjaro so far, I have never had a problem because I observe my guests closely and avoid putting anyone at risk.

Kilimanjaro is a fun climb that, with a bit of care, is very safe. Each morning we do an individual medical checklist for each guest: pulse oxygen saturation[26], Diamox[27], and in general how they are feeling. We also make sure they are eating, sleeping, and going to the bathroom normally. I find that taking this time to reassure my guests that they are doing fine is important to their mental wellbeing.

---

26 A measurement of the oxygen saturation of arterial blood in a person by utilizing a sensor attached typically to a finger, toe, or ear; used to determine the percentage of oxyhemoglobin in blood.
27 **Diamox** is a carbonic anhydrase inhibitor that is used as a medical aid for altitude acclimatization.

Because guides must push people up against their limits but not beyond them, a guide must be attuned to each person's individual needs and abilities. Some may be experienced climbers; others may be on their first big adventure like this. This is especially true of a trip like Kilimanjaro that draws both veteran and new climbers. Recognizing that every person on a climb is different helps you custom-tailor guiding techniques appropriate to each person's circumstances. A seasoned climber needs a different kind of motivation than someone above 16,000 feet for the first time. I find that people often hit some walls when they ascend above 16,000 feet and beyond—the point at which the body is slowly adjusting to the altitude and people generally start to feel uncomfortable.

For this reason, custom tailoring your guiding experience to each individual is crucial to good guiding. One of my most memorable trips up Kilimanjaro was with a couple—Art Ulene and his wife, Priscilla—who were both in their seventies at the time. In order to guide them up the mountain I had to pay special attention to their needs and limits, but at the same time I didn't want to underestimate them or sell them short. I wanted to be sure we did everything we could to get them to the top of Kilimanjaro and back down safely, as with any other guest.

Art had worked as a medical advisor for *NBC* for twenty-three years. All his life, he has been an ambitious man who had set goals and accomplished them. He is always pushing himself—searching for the edge of his comfort zone and pushing just past it. For his seventy-fifth birthday, he wanted to summit Kilimanjaro. By the time a mutual friend referred him to me, several other agencies had already refused to take him up due to his age. Most guides were not up for the challenge of guiding someone his age. In order to make it work, I agreed to guide him and his wife, just the three of us and some porters, on a custom-private World Wide Trekking trip. This way I could tailor the trip to their needs and their needs alone.

Normally, I have a very set routine when it comes to guiding people up Kilimanjaro. On most trips, I take people up to the summit over the course of seven or eight days, depending upon the route taken. In the case of Art and Priscilla, I decided to spread it out over nine days. Given their age, I knew they would travel more slowly than my typical groups. With age, people tend not to bounce back as quickly from heavy exertion, so I gave us two extra days to go slowly, acclimate fully, and pace ourselves appropriately. And we planned the trip so that our summit day would be on Art's birthday.

This was to be my fourth climb of Kilimanjaro that season. Art and Priscilla flew into Tanzania as I was coming off the mountain from my previous trip. We met up and started to prepare. Everything went off without a hitch, and we got to the mountain on schedule. In order to accommodate Art and Priscilla's slower pace, I planned the trek differently than I would plan a typical World Wide Trekking trip. Rather than staying at the normal camps, we would sometimes be stopping and throwing up tents between camps.

The first day went as expected. We were moving slowly but steadily. I wasn't quite confident yet that we would make it to the summit for Art's birthday (or perhaps at all), but Art and Priscilla were enjoying every moment of the trip. They are the type of people who love life and the natural world, and they were always stopping to observe the interesting flora and fauna you find as you move up through Kilimanjaro's separate ecological zones. Kilimanjaro can be very cold at night and warm during the day, and this has forced the plant and animal life to struggle to adapt, and caused it to evolve in interesting ways.

On the second morning, I began to notice that Art and Priscilla weren't recovering as fast as younger climbers tend to. I had expected this, but I hadn't anticipated that this would make it difficult to estimate exactly how far we would travel each day. This made planning hard. We simply had to fall into whatever pace we could, and go as far as we could safely move in a day.

On the fifth night, I was lying alone in my tent thinking about our progress. I couldn't sleep. I was worried about Art and Priscilla, who were beginning to look tired. Knowing what would come as we entered into higher altitudes, I wanted to be sure we could make the top. They were dragging more and more each day, looking more and more tired out. I was afraid that we weren't going to make it to the summit if we kept up our current pace. They needed more time to make it to the top, and if they didn't get more time, they were going to exhaust themselves and get sick and have to come back down. I was pretty certain this was how it would play out if we continued at this pace, but I was hesitant to turn back: Art really wanted to summit, and I really wanted him to be able to realize that goal. The guide in me didn't want to turn back unless we absolutely had to, but I also didn't want to set us up to fail.

I didn't sleep well that night. I knew that we had to change our plan, whether it was convenient or not, and I resolved to do so. I had always thought of my seven-day plan as foolproof, and by allowing two extra days, I thought I had given us enough of a buffer to summit. But my buffer wasn't adequate—I could see that now. My first time guiding seniors was presenting challenges I hadn't expected. I knew Art would be disappointed not to summit on his birthday, but this was still better than not summiting at all.

In the morning, I went to their tent. "We need to change plans,"

I told them. "If we keep proceeding like this, we aren't going to make the summit. You're getting more worn down every day. If we keep on, we might come close to the summit, but we won't get there. So here is what we need to do. We need to take a really short day today. We are going to walk for an hour or two only, then set up camp early. I want you guys to take off the afternoon, just sleep in your tent. You need to rest and recover before we push on."

As always, Art and Priscilla put full faith in my decision. I am lucky to have groups that value my decisions and experience—they are generally looking to me to guide them. Art and Priscilla were no different. They trusted me to get them up and down the mountain safely.

At this point, my crew began to question how slowly we were moving. They didn't understand why we would hike two hours out of camp only to set a new camp there. I explained that the reason was that we needed to pace ourselves according to Art and Priscilla. We needed to focus not only on how fast we were currently moving, but how fast we would be able to move in the future. Going too fast at this stage was tiring them out. If we kept it up, they were going to be too tired to summit when the time came. Every step we took toward the top brought us closer to the goal—but it also exhausted them. A day resting in the tent was just what they needed in order to be able to pull this off. That was what *they* needed—not every single climber, but these particular two. Thankfully, my crew (the best Kili-crew in the world, in my opinion) understood the logic behind my changes to the itinerary.

After taking that day to recover, we were able to proceed with my plan. We were moving more slowly than we had been—maybe even more slowly than we had to—but Art and Priscilla were now moving at a pace that would allow them to keep going for the long haul. For my part, I was again feeling good about our chance of making a successful summit bid. It looked like we were all going to accomplish our goals after all!

We made our way slowly up the mountain. We had found a pace that was working for us, and we kept to it. Each day, I made sure that Art and Priscilla were good to go before pushing on. On the seventh day we reached our highest camp, which put us within summiting distance.

This was the most crucial part of the climb, and it is the hardest part of climbing Kilimanjaro. The summit night is when most people start doubting themselves. This is when I really have to encourage and motivate people. I have to make them believe in themselves. When they want to give up, I tell them, "No, no, no. Let's just take a break. We'll slow it down a little bit. Then we'll keep going." When people start struggling or losing spirit, you have to step in and motivate them. You have to remind them that they can indeed do this. I don't let guests give up easily. If I conceded every time someone said they couldn't go any further, I wouldn't have such a high success rate, and neither would my guests. But I do, and so do they, because I step in and remind them that they can do this.

Art and Priscilla were definitely struggling near the top, but they were also having a good time. I could tell they believed they could make it, and I believed they could. We had been very careful to stay in tiptop shape in preparation for this day.

Most climbers like to time the summit so that they can hit the top right at sunrise. The sun comes over the glacier, causing the ice to glisten, and the view is spectacular. But to make the summit by sunrise, you have to set out from camp the evening before and climb all night in the dark and cold. I was pretty sure that wasn't going to work for Art and Priscilla. On the last leg of Kilimanjaro, from

> **Most climbers like to time the summit so that they can hit the top right at sunrise. The sun comes over the glacier, causing the ice to glisten, and the view is spectacular.**

16,000 feet upward, the altitude begins to change the environment. Gone are the jungles and alpine deserts. The air becomes thin and cold, and the terrain icy and barren. At night, it can get quite cold. In order to enable Art and Priscilla to summit during the night, we would have had to take many breaks for them to stop and warm up. I wasn't sure that we would have even been able to make it to the top like that.

In order to make it to the summit, we had to again diverge from the standard plan. We didn't leave camp until after 3:00 in the morning, much later than we would wake if we were trying to summit by sunrise. Within another hour or two we were on our way to the summit. We continued to set our own pace. It was almost noon by the time we made it up onto Uhuru Peak.[28] The sun was out and high in the sky and it was much warmer than it would have been at sunrise, which made it much easier on Art and Priscilla, who had been showing signs of being excessively cold even at lower altitudes.

We climbed throughout the day until we finally reached the summit. We had done it. *They* had done it. We stood on top of Kilimanjaro, looking down into the dormant crater. Art was seventy-five years old and one day, and Priscilla was seventy-three years old. It was inspiring to see them realize their goal. As far as I know, they were the oldest couple ever to have summited Kilimanjaro together

---

28 Uhuru Peak is the highest summit on Kibo's crater rim, and the highest point on Kilimanjaro at 19,340 feet.

at the time. Art and his wife are amazing people, and they proved it up on that mountain. I just hope that I am still climbing when I turn seventy-five. They are both still good friends of mine, and we climb together almost every year now. They inspire me, and I think back on that first climb often.

For my part, I was proud to have helped them see it through. Again, that's one of the greatest joys as a guide, and the true essence of guiding—taking pride in other people's success. Your goal as a guide is to help them meet their goals. When they succeed, you succeed. When they got back down again on the tenth day, I knew that we had all met our goals. They had done their part, and I had done mine. We had succeeded together.

This is why I guide. It is why I will continue to guide. I don't need to see the summit of Kilimanjaro forty times, but I will never get tired of helping people push themselves to their limits. Every year I take more groups up to Kilimanjaro. These groups have about a dozen people each. Each person is different, with different motivations and skills. This always presents new challenges because, everyone being different, you have to tailor your guiding to fit your guests each time. Art and Priscilla may have been an extreme case, being much older than most of my guests, but everyone is always different. In a way, the trip with Art and Priscilla was easier than some other trips because, since it was just the three of us, I could change plans for them without affecting anyone else.

CHAPTER SEVEN

Cotopaxi:
The Journey Is the Thing

"Focus on the journey, not the destination.
Joy is found not in finishing an activity but in doing it."
—Greg Anderson

My wife, Alison, and I had something of a whirlwind romance. We met in June 2008, and by the following April, we were married. This probably seems borderline insane to some people, and I might have agreed before I met Alison, but we hit it off really well and just knew. We shared our love of the outdoors and adventure: We met when she came on one of my Kilimanjaro trips, and at the end of the trip we made plans to meet up in Switzerland to do some hiking and sightseeing.

After the wedding was over, we wanted to go on a long getaway together before the climbing season started and I got busy guiding for my business. Some people spend their honeymoon at Niagara Falls, or in Vegas, or on a beach somewhere in Hawaii. Not us—we went mountain climbing in Ecuador. We planned to climb Cotopaxi, the world's tallest active volcano by many accounts.[29]

---

29 Some consider Cotopaxi the world's tallest active volcano, but others give this distinction to the considerably taller Llullaillaco in Chile, which most recently erupted in 1877.

This was pretty typical fare for us. We had gone on climbs together in Tanzania, and Alison had come with me to Machu Picchu. We had hiked all over Snowbird and Utah. We half-jokingly called these trips "super dates." So she was no novice to trekking, climbing, or the outdoors. That said, she had never been on a climb that would require glacier gear, such as crampons, ice axes, and ropes for safe travel. This gear takes training and practice to use effectively.

We would need this gear. Cotopaxi is a volcano that is snowcapped all year around. Crampons and ice axes are not optional on the glacier. This was something Alison had no experience with. She had been on higher elevation mountains, including Kilimanjaro, but she had never made such a high-altitude technical climb. I didn't doubt her ability to tackle Cotopaxi, but I knew we would have to warm up, get her well acclimatized, and do some training to get her up to speed on how to use crampons and ropes. It was going to be the kind of experience that would take her outside her comfort zone and test her limits. (What a way to spend your honeymoon, right? Maybe *now* you think we're crazy?)

All of this training and preparation aside, we knew one thing—we were there to have fun. This was about spending time together as a young married couple pursuing the things we both loved—specifically, adventure.

We planned a full itinerary. If we were going to climb Cotopaxi, which stood at a height of 19,347 feet, we would need to acclimatize first. Rather than go up and down the same mountain several times, we thought it would be fun to climb two lower peaks in the same area. We also planned to spend some time in the local communities to have fun off the mountain as well.

Our first stop was Quito, the capital of Ecuador. Quito is situated on the slopes of the Andes, and at 9,350, is the highest official capital city in the world. We visited the stunning old town district and stopped at the markets and shops. We stopped by the Plaza Grande. We toured stunning cathedrals from the fifteenth century. It was a great time, and chance to unwind before going up the mountain, which was why we there in the first place—to unwind and have fun.

The next day we took the *TelefériQo*, an aerial tramway that takes you from the center of town up to the slopes of Pichincha, a mountain just outside Quito. From the tram, you can see the city spread out below you and the peak of the mountain up above. The tram took us up to about 12,000 feet, and from there we climbed to the top of Pichincha at 15,444 feet. This was an acclimatization day, to prepare us for Cotopaxi. It is also a fun climb. You have to scramble up rocks to get to the summit. It was early in the season, which meant there were few people on the mountain. Despite the season not having really kicked in, we were blessed with wonderful weather.

We came back down and spent the night in Quito. The next day, we took a shuttle bus to Chilcabamba Lodge, an eco lodge just outside of Cotopaxi National Park, where we spent the night. The lodge was amazing. The staff spoke only Spanish, and the very walls seemed to exude local culture. The lodge was mostly empty this early in the season, so we basically had the place to ourselves—what more can you ask for on a honeymoon getaway? Our room had a fireplace and a stunning view of Cotopaxi—the mountain rising in a perfect, pointed volcanic cone, beautifully snowcapped with the crater at the top visible from a distance.

I couldn't wait to get up the mountain, but we had more acclimatizing to do first. The next day we took a break from climbing to go horseback riding in the park, but the day after that we climbed Sincholagua, a 16,000-foot inactive volcano near Cotopaxi. As before, the weather was perfect, the trails and slopes weren't crowded, and we had a fantastic time yet again.

The next day we reserved for resting up at the lodge before tackling Cotopaxi. We spent a little time doing some last-minute training: I taught Alison how to tie ropes, move in crampons, and self-arrest with an ice axe to prevent herself from sliding down the glacier. We went outside to practice them. She looked a little awkward and uncomfortable in the crampons, but she soon got the hang of them.

The following morning, we caught a ride into Cotopaxi National Park, strapped on our gear, and hiked up to Refugio, a stone mountain hut that climbers can use for shelter in lieu of having to set up a camp. We stayed in the bunkroom there and hired a cook. I spent the rest of the afternoon on the glacier with Alison, doing more training with ropes and crampons. Having never used crampons, she needed practice walking with them on actual ice before trying it at higher altitudes.

Then we got some rest that evening. We planned to head out at about midnight so that we could push to the summit by sunrise and then descend again before the slopes started to melt and become more active—and thus treacherous—in the later afternoon. Now fully acclimated, we were ready to make a push straight to the top with no stops.

We set out from Refugio shortly after midnight as planned, and climbed throughout the night. The weather and ice conditions were good, and it was fun climbing, even in the dark. As we neared the top, the sun started to come up, making the mountain beautiful.

Unfortunately, we were starting to run into problems at about this time. Alison was starting to move noticeably slower, and the stress from wearing crampons was hurting her ankles and lower legs. The spikes put an immense amount of pressure on your legs as they dig into the ice, and it can be painful if you aren't accustomed to wearing them. The strain was visibly fatiguing her.

Normally in this situation, with any other person, I would have told them to stop and give their muscles a break before pushing on. Crampons can be hard on the legs if you don't have the best form and aren't used to them, but most people can suffer through the discomfort. Certainly, Alison could. She was strong, athletic, and spirited. Yes, it would be uncomfortable, but then again, pushing yourself beyond your comfort zone usually is!

I asked her if she was all right. She said she was, and so, after a short break, we pushed on toward the summit. She wasn't okay, though. We had to keep stopping to give her legs a break. We were getting close to the last steep section of the climb, which leads up to the summit ridge, but we still had a ways to go. The climb to the top isn't super technical, but it is a scramble over ice to get to the top, and the pain in her legs was getting worse.

We stopped to rest again. Alison was starting to look miserable. We were so close to the summit though … if we just pushed on a little more, I knew we could make it to the top. But then it hit me: looking at Alison, I could see she was no longer having fun. And that was what we had come here for in the first place. This wasn't some hardcore mountain climbing trip. It was our honeymoon, and she had reached the point at which this was no longer fun.

With a guest on an expedition, I would have just said, "Look, let's take an even longer break and push on." But she wasn't a guest, and this wasn't a paid adventure tour. We weren't here to conquer the mountain. It was our honeymoon, and we were here to have fun. Or at least, we had been.

"Hey, Alison," I said. "Let's just go back down. We've had enough, right?"

She thought about it for a moment. I could tell she was reluctant to turn back. We *both* wanted to summit (for a long time afterward, she would refer to the climb as her white whale), but this wasn't the right day for it. We could almost certainly make it to the top, but doing so was going to sap the day of any fun. We would end up with a bad memory instead of a good one. That's not the way you're supposed to spend your honeymoon.

Alison agreed. We had nothing to prove here, and it really had stopped being fun with her in so much pain. We turned back, having never summited, having never stood at the summit ridge and looked down into the crater. I knew there was a chance we might never come back there again—but it didn't matter. That wasn't why we were there, and it wasn't why we were on a honeymoon. We'd lost sight of the forest for the trees; we'd lost sight of the journey for the summit.

The decision was a good one. Alison started to feel better as we moved back into lower elevations. We were moving more slowly, and gravity was now on our side. The weather was nice on the way down, and this made for easier movement and an enjoyable climb down the mountain, which made wearing the crampons easier on

Alison. Once we got off the glacier, we could take them off and just climb and hike normally. We were again in good spirits. We stopped along the way to rest and talk. We took photos. We were again enjoying our honeymoon and each other, the very thing we had set out to do in the first place.

Life is not about the destination; it's about the journey. Enjoy the journey!

Life is not about the destination; it's about the journey. Enjoy the journey!

CHAPTER EIGHT

Cho Oyu:
The Five Hazardous Attitudes and Breaking the Chain

"You can't connect the dots looking forward; you can only connect them looking backwards. So you have to trust that the dots will somehow connect in your future. You have to trust in something—your gut, destiny, life, karma, whatever. Because believing that the dots will connect down the road will give you the confidence to follow your heart, even when it leads you off the well-worn path."
—Steve Jobs

In 2010, I agreed to guide a private client on Cho Oyu. This would be his first time at an elevation above 8,000 meters. In the climbing community, much is made of the "eight-thousanders," the peaks that rise to this height. They represent a true challenge, because once you proceed beyond about 8,000 meters and into the death zone, the human body can no longer completely acclimatize to the reduction in pressure and available oxygen. Acclimatization is necessary even to enter the death zone, but no level of acclimatization will ever allow you to remain there indefinitely. The human body was simply not meant to remain in such extreme environments.

There are only fourteen eight-thousander peaks in the world, and all of them are in the Himalayan and Karakoram mountain ranges in Asia. At 26,906 feet, Cho Oyu is the sixth highest mountain in the world. It is also widely regarded as the most forgiving of all the eight-thousanders due to the non-technical nature of the climb.

That said, Cho Oyu is in no way an "easy" climb to be taken lightly. Nothing is easy at 8,000 meters. The effects of altitude at these heights make climbing that would be easy at lower altitudes an ordeal. There is also weather to contend with, and the usual mountain dangers. Climbers die on Cho Oyu every year, usually due to falls or avalanches. There aren't many steep cliffs to traverse, but the entire route is a trudge up steep, snow-laden slopes, which is taxing at this altitude. These challenges make Cho Oyu a good training ground for testing your skills and mettle before heading up Mt Everest or one of the other, less forgiving eight-thousanders. Cho Oyu allows you a taste of the death zone to see how your body reacts before you attempt technical climbing at such an extreme altitude.

As with my client, this was also my first and only time up on Cho Oyu. We met up in Kathmandu as part of a larger climbing expedition. There were about eight climbers in all, plus Sherpas, but I was guiding him privately, by myself.

Almost immediately, we began running into problems. As with all of the eight-thousanders, a successful summit bid is largely dependent upon the weather. Unfortunately, it had been raining and snowing on the mountain for months. By the time we got up to Base Camp—taking a slow, week-long approach in order to acclimatize en route—the conditions were terrible due to the fresh snow, which put us at high risk for avalanche activity. There had been a number of big incidents involving avalanches on the mountain that year, several of which involved climbers who were taken out by a slide and had to be rescued.

These kinds of accidents happen frequently on big mountains. You have to stay focused on what you can control, and not let accidents distract you. The main thing is to just be cautious. Practice good decision-making, focus on the basics, weigh the consequences of your actions carefully, and be ready to change your plans if conditions on the mountain change. These good practices are what keep you safe. I was sure they would now keep us safe on Cho Oyu in what was a particularly active year on the mountain (this year brought lots of active avalanches, and snowfall), or so I thought. I was sure that, despite the harsh conditions, my training, experience, and caution would keep us safe and see us to the top.

The weather was too bad to make a summit bid anytime soon, but we set about climbing up and down the mountain to acclimate. We moved slowly from Base Camp up to Camp I to get my client acclimated. I am blessed with the ability to acclimatize very quickly to altitude, but this varies among people. The best way to handle acclimatization is to climb up high on the mountain and then come back down to camp and rest, each day going a little higher. On very big mountains, going up near the highest elevations often means coming back all the way down to Base Camp to rest before going up any further or making a summit push.

We spent three weeks on the mountain, acclimating by moving back and forth between Base Camp, Camp I, and Camp II. However, hazardous weather conditions were affecting the upper part of the mountain. Above Camp II, the conditions were too hazardous to venture higher due to avalanche danger. The snow kept falling, day after day, and avalanches continued to trigger. There was nothing to do but patiently wait the weather out.

All this time up at high altitude was taking a toll on my client, who started having trouble with altitude sickness. For the better part of a week, he had been suffering from near constant nausea and headaches. He wasn't experiencing cerebral or pulmonary edema, just acute mountain sickness (AMS). The worst part was that the AMS kept him from sleeping, which further fatigued him. He was moving slowly on climbing days, and he was starting to lose the motivation it would take to get to the top.

Prior to this, we had both felt great; we were climbing well and pushing ourselves hard up and down the mountain. Sometimes all you need to kick AMS is to go down lower on the mountain and rest up. We tried going back down to Base Camp to rest at 15,500 feet. Unfortunately, he wasn't fully recovering, even when we stopped there. When this happens, altitude sickness tends to progress and get worse the longer you are on the mountain. I knew that the longer we stayed on the mountain, the worse he would get. His headaches would intensify, and he would get clumsy as his motor skills and reaction time deteriorated—which can be dangerous. The mountains are difficult even on a good day. If you are going to succeed on a big mountain climb, you need to be at your best, feeling strong and capable so that you can push yourself.

After resting at Base Camp, we took another stab at the mountain, moving from Base Camp back up to Camp I to position ourselves on the mountain in case the weather suddenly got better. By the time the snow cleared enough for us to make a try at Camp II, my client had begun to get very sick. He had been in bad shape for over a week now, and it was only getting worse. I tried to motivate him and keep him positive, but he was starting to falter, and for good reason. Altitude sickness is a miserable feeling, and it can be quite dangerous if you ignore it.

At this point he came to me and said, "You know, Dean, I think I'm done. I'm ready to go home. I can't do this right now."

I could tell he didn't want to go, that he really wanted to make it up—but it just wasn't going to happen. Normally, I try to talk people into toughing it out, but only when it is safe to do so. I was not about to dissuade him at that point.

The whole thing was disappointing for me. I had put substantial time into doing the climb, and I really wanted to summit. This was my first time on Cho Oyu. I didn't know if I would ever be back. The opportunity to climb some mountains may only come once in a lifetime, and walking away then seemed like such a shame. I was fully acclimated. I felt good. If the weather would just clear, I could have started for the summit right then. I told myself that at some point the snow would surely have to settle down long enough for me to make a summit bid.

I was thinking about all of this as we packed up our gear to head back down. I decided that I wanted to continue the climb alone after accompanying him down the mountain. I asked him if that would be okay.

"Yeah," he said. "I want you to stay."

I arranged for my Nepal operations manager, Geljen, to take him back to Kathmandu. I walked my guest down off the mountain and accompanied him on the one-day walk to the place where he could get a ride. The following day, I made my way back to Base Camp, where I rested for a day before making my way up to Camp I. From there I started my push back up the mountain alone.

I was up on the mountain for another week after my guest left. I made it all the way up to the high camp, but had to come back down due to the weather. I was trying to position myself for my summit bid, but I couldn't hit a window that would work. The weather wouldn't clear, and the mountain wouldn't let me up. It wasn't just me—the mountain wasn't letting *anyone* up, and most climbers had packed up and left. I had told myself that the weather had to turn at some point, but the snow continued to fall off and on. Even when the snow stopped, it was still too hazardous up high on the mountain. The fresh snow was sensitive, just waiting for a trigger that would send it coming down off the upper slopes.

One night I was up at Camp II, alone in my tent. I was cold; now that my client was gone and it was just me, there was only one body making heat. I lay there in my bag, trying to keep warm, making water from a stove hung from the top of my tent. I could hear the winds and the snow blowing relentlessly outside. Doubt was beginning to set in. I started to wonder if it was even safe to be up on the mountain alone like this, in these conditions. I imagined an avalanche coming down the slope above me and burying me in my tent. Who would dig me out? I thought about my wife, Alison, and how she was expecting me home.

Put simply: I was having serious reservations about continuing, and yet that was exactly what I was doing.

Ultimately, I pushed these thoughts out of my mind, dismissing them as negative thinking. What I needed to do was to keep my eye on the goal, not wallow in negativity. I told myself, *be patient, slow down, let the mountain settle down—and then you will go up.* I thought about the big picture, reminding myself that the mountain would decide what happened. It was up to me to work with her. I had to push my limits, but not push too far too fast.

On the following morning, as I was preparing to set out to the next camp and on to the final push, another large slide came down the mountain. The avalanche took out a party of four climbers, who then had to be rescued. This was a major accident that forced me all the way back down to Base Camp. The slopes were just too active to be up on the mountain; I could see that now. I wondered, *is this the mountain telling me to go down?*

This may seem myopic or irrational to others, as there had been other fatal accidents on the mountain before this one. But this time I had been *on* the mountain, just down a little lower. It is much easier to distance yourself from an accident when you aren't there to see it or hear about it firsthand. You know that there are lots of accidents on big mountains—you hear about them all the time—but you try not to focus on them. You have to keep your attention on the things that you can control.

However, this doesn't mean that you push blindly forward no matter what. If accidents are telling you that it is too hazardous on the mountain, you need to listen. This accident brought things into focus and sharpened my perspective on my situation. This was when it hit me—what in the hell was I doing? Cho Oyu was not safe right then. Being there alone was doubly unsafe. No one had made it up the mountain that year because the weather wouldn't allow it. This was *not* negativity—it was reality. I should have been reassessing my goals, not risking my life. That could very easily have been me taken out by the avalanche that morning. My desire to summit had blinded me to the risks I was taking. I should have turned back, but instead I had made the terrible decision to press on.

Training materials put out by the Federal Aviation Administration

Training materials put out by the Federal Aviation Administration (FAA) warn against five hazardous attitudes that can negatively affect a pilot's decision-making process.

(FAA) warn against five hazardous attitudes that can negatively affect a pilot's decision-making process. These materials were formulated to help train pilots in aeronautical decision-making, but they can help all people improve their decision-making prowess, which is why they have become so popular. I am an ardent believer in watching out for the five hazardous attitudes, and I have at various times seen all five of them in myself.

The five hazardous attitudes are: resignation, antiauthority, impulsivity, invulnerability, and machismo, the latter of which I and others prefer to call overconfidence. They are all basically what they sound like.

1. *Resignation* means giving up too easily and assuming that the outcome of a situation is due to chance.

2. *Antiauthority* refers to a know-it-all attitude and a refusal to defer to others who have more experience with or knowledge of the situation.

3. *Impulsivity* refers to unnecessarily quick decision-making that arises from a lack of patience.

4. *Invulnerability*, often a hazard of youth but certainly not confined to the young, is an attitude that ignores risks and assumes (incorrectly) that something can never happen to you.

5. Finally, *overconfidence*—an attitude all too prevalent among outdoor enthusiasts and adventure-seekers—results in unnecessary risk-taking.

This may all seem obvious—the five hazardous attitudes are easy to explain and understand. But they are far less easy to identify in the moment, which is what makes them so detrimental to sound decision-making. They keep you from recognizing your own decision-making errors. In essence, they mask themselves. To overcome this, you have to learn to watch out for them and actively break the chain of hazardous thinking.

While on Cho Oyu, I was very aware of the five hazardous attitudes, but I didn't realize that I was exhibiting many of them. I had impulsively decided to go up the mountain alone, ignoring the risks. I made this decision out of a feeling of invulnerability and overconfidence—it wasn't until an avalanche took out four other climbers that I realized, *Wait, this really could happen to me!*

The thing is: the mountain doesn't know you are an expert. It doesn't know you have training. The mountain doesn't have feelings and it doesn't care. That's not to say that training isn't important, but training will only do you so much good when a wall of snow comes crashing down and buries you and your tent several feet deep.

I always say, when the mountain pushes you, *push back*. I believe this to be the key to self-motivation. However, you also have to recognize when it's time to call it quits and respect what the mountain is telling you. And it was clear to me that the mountain was telling me to leave. I had been blinding myself to that message due to the five hazardous attitudes.

The trick to overcoming the five hazardous attitudes is constant attention. It took a major accident to snap me to my senses and remind me that I wasn't invincible, and to make me realize I was taking unnecessary and imprudent risks. I was lucky—that avalanche could have hit me. Don't take chances like that due to errors in judgment. Look for these attitudes in yourself when you are making decisions, especially critical ones. Don't get complacent, and do think about the consequences of your actions. Ask yourself always:

am I making this decision because it is the right one, or is there a hazardous thought process steering me astray here?

Once you recognize one of the attitudes in yourself, you need to break the chain. Sometimes, this can be relatively easy, as when a large avalanche comes down and takes out people around you. Sometimes, however, breaking the chain can be more difficult. It takes a lot of courage to admit that you are acting impulsively or being anti-authoritarian, but it is necessary in order to clear your thought processes and eliminate negative, dangerous attitudes that are preventing you from making safe, sound decisions in life. Be diligent about breaking the chain. You have to be continuously aware of the hazardous attitudes and always looking for them. Be mindful of them.

> **Be diligent about breaking the chain. You have to be continuously aware of the hazardous attitudes and always looking for them. Be mindful of them.**

The fact is that many of the hazardous attitudes are really just positive, helpful, personal qualities taken to the extreme. You don't want to be impulsive, but you do want to act quickly. You don't want to be antiauthoritarian, but you do want to trust your gut and yourself. You don't want to be overconfident or act like you're invulnerable, but neither should you be meek or too scared to push back at obstacles. You don't want to be resigned, but you do want to be realistic about your situation, as was the case for me up on Cho Oyu, when the mountain was telling me it wasn't safe and it was time to turn back.

Finding that balance between pushing forward confidently and knowing when it is appropriate to turn back—and striking a balance with the other hazardous attitudes—requires experience, mindfulness, practice, and careful attention to detail. It requires you to always be assessing and reassessing where you are, what you're doing, and the specific circumstances you are confronting.

CHAPTER NINE

World Wide Trekking :
Taking You Outside Your Comfort Zone

"Risk more than others think is safe,
care more than others think is wise,
dream more than others think is practical,
expect more than others think is possible."
—Cadet Maxim

Much of this book has been dedicated to sharing stories of my mountain adventures and the lessons learned from them. I hope some of what I have written here helps you push yourself outside your comfort zone. That doesn't mean you have to climb the world's tallest mountains or go on outdoor adventures that last for several months at a time. These lessons are applicable to everyday life off the mountain, too. You don't have to scale Everest to make use of concepts like situational awareness, perseverance, methodical planning, completing goals in increments, knowing when to get back to basics, or any of the others presented in this book. These lessons will aid you not just on the mountain, but also in everyday life. I know this because they have done so for me.

In no area of my life has this been truer than in the launching of my business, World Wide Trekking (WWTrek). I started my business in 2006 as a one-man operation in my employee dorm room at Snowbird. I spent my days off working on launching my business. The business has since grown into an international company with multiple employees and dozens and dozens of contractors around the world. We have even established a nonprofit arm. Best of all, I get to wake up each day and do something I love while helping others push themselves beyond their own self-imposed limits. I don't know that I could have accomplished any of this without the lessons I learned on those mountains.

I never set out to start a company, not at first. I just wanted to guide my own trips. I had been guiding for two decades and never thought of it as an actual career so much as a job I enjoyed that allowed me to go on amazing adventures. I loved the work, but working for other agencies could be frustrating. For example, trips would sometimes fall through, wreaking havoc on my schedule. Service was sometimes second-rate, which frustrated my guests and me. What frustrated me the most were the operational methods of many other guide services. Time and time again, I thought, *I could do better.* Eventually I asked myself, *Why don't I?*

People I met at Snowbird, having heard about some of the exciting adventures I had been on, often asked me to guide them, so I started planning my own trips in 2006. I set up a climb on Kilimanjaro for a group of people who had asked me to guide them, and we had more people than would fit on one trip, so we scheduled a second. Then another group expressed interest in doing a trek to the Mount Everest Base Camp, and a private guest wanted me to take him up Mount Elbrus in Russia.

None of this was planned. I wasn't drawing up itineraries. It was just me agreeing to guide acquaintances and their friends. I saw an opportunity though, and I seized it. Success in life is often dependent upon recognizing the opportunities in front of you. I may not have set out to found a company doing what I love, but I jumped at the opportunity to do so.

> Success in life is often dependent upon recognizing the opportunities in front of you.

At that point, it was just a matter of putting my nose to the grindstone. In the evenings I stayed cloistered in my dorm room, working on the business. I hashed out a logo, drew up some itineraries, networked to find vendors and staff, and tried to put together those first trips. By spring of 2007, I started running the first trips. We did about four trips that first season.

Those early years were tough, especially the first. I definitely made some beginner mistakes and hit major setbacks, such as picking bad flight routes and doing suboptimal scheduling. Eager to get everything ready beforehand, I would often fly into a destination too early and spend a week waiting for my guests and crew to arrive, blowing through money needlessly the whole time.

The biggest challenge was finding the right people to work with. When working in remote areas of faraway countries, you have to hire local people to handle money and logistics for you. You need people you can trust, and who can also trust you. This is important when working half a world away and booking reservations months in advance. Trust takes time to build, and starting out without this foundation was difficult. Nonetheless, I was regularly wiring money to people on the other side of the world whom I might never see again. This happened frequently at first. I had one guide in Tanzania who worked with me for the first two years, and then just vanished along with all of our tents.

The worst case happened in my very first year. I hired the same subcontractor to handle logistics for two Kilimanjaro treks. The first trip went off fine, but then he went missing. The day before the guests were scheduled to arrive, I finally got in touch with him. The news wasn't good—he told me he wasn't coming. It wasn't until later that I found out he had fled because he had mismanaged our money and skipped town after failing to pay some of our staff.

I was extremely disappointed—mostly for my guests. I had ten guests flying in the next day, and no staff. But I refused to throw in the towel or let our guests down. I called around until I found another guy, an acquaintance from guiding, to help me coordinate logistics, get permits, and assemble a mountain crew. This guy managed to assemble a staff of sixty-five people overnight! This was practically impossible, but he made it happen. There were a few hiccups, and we had to wing some things, but the trip was a total success.

Unfortunately, things took a turn for the worse when we came off the mountain. The hotel told us that they didn't have our reservation—the absentee subcontractor had canceled the reservation and disappeared with the refund. This was a substantial loss that had the potential to sink the business.

We could have folded right then and there, cutting our losses and running, but we didn't. The guests had paid, and we had to make it right for the guests. We called around and booked new rooms at an equally good lodge. As for the money, it was gone. I had to eat the loss. This was a devastating financial blow, but we survived it. This taught me the secret to sound customer service: Whatever happens, you make it right for the guest. We promise the guests a certain experience, and we have to deliver. Everything else is secondary.

Things were hard that first year. We barely broke even. But at the end of the day, I was just happy to have a business doing what I loved. With patience, I continued to grow the business, and eventually things started to get better. I learned more about running a business, and I got better at dealing with guests, vendors, the local guys, and all the other facets of the business. I learned the best places to stay, and made contacts that got WWTrek better deals. We made friends in the local communities, establishing mutual trust and goodwill.

The business needed constant attention. I labored happily over our itineraries, always adjusting them to match our guests' interests. We wanted our trips to be the best possible, each one a totally personalized success story. It wasn't enough for me just to copy what everyone else was doing. I worked hard to make our trips different—unique even.

The most important thing was finding the right people to work with. I now have a whole outfit of people in various locations—particularly in Nepal, Peru, and Tanzania, where we visit often—all of whom I trust and have been working with for years. They share my passion for people, experiences, and places. World Wide Trekking aims to deliver the best possible experience whether or not I personally guide your trip.

I was only able to pull this off by hiring close friends. My employees aren't just local guys; they are local guys I have worked with, guided with, and traveled with. They are my friends. In the early days I didn't have bank accounts set up overseas, so I had to carry cash to pay or wire funds at the last minute. I couldn't trust wiring money to early to people I had not worked with before. I have since built long-standing relationships with my overseas operations managers, and they are my close friends and work partners.

With the right people in place, I no longer have to fly around with thousands of dollars taped in bundles to my thighs in order to pay reservations at the last minute in cash! We set up overseas bank accounts and even established locally licensed businesses that could operate in the places we traveled to frequently. We also established relations with vendors and the greater local communities. People we visit in the teahouses in Nepal smile when they see us, both because we bring them business and because we are genuinely their friends. We have worked hard to build this mutual trust. It's all about treating people with respect—be they guests, local community members, hotel workers, guides, Sherpas, or whoever. We try to leave a lasting, positive impression on everyone.

These human relationships are my greatest asset as a businessperson. From the start, I have run my business not by the numbers, but from the heart. This means treating people right. It means paying my workers well and treating them with dignity. It means always making it right for the guest. It means honoring the values of the community and giving back as much as you can. When you open your heart and give as much as you can, you receive the same in kind. At the end of the day, all businesses are people businesses. Businesses thrive when they focus on people.

I've always been drawn to guiding by my desire to experience new places, new things, and especially new *people*. Those are the reasons I left my family's engineering firm and moved to Utah. Those are the reasons I loved being a guide and a teacher. Those are the reasons I founded World Wide Trekking. I wanted to bring people together to share amazing experiences, and the most amazing experience of all is the shared human experience. The most rewarding aspect of the business is making new lifelong friends of our guides, community members, business partners, and of course, our guests, many of whom are repeat guests who have become true friends.

As the company grows, I try to hew closely to this original intent. I remind myself that I didn't start this just for money, but to pursue what I love and to share that with other people.

We have come a long way, and we have a long way to go. We always will. World Wide Trekking was founded with the intent of doing things better, and we strive to live up to that mission every day. From the beginning I knew I wanted to create a high-end service providing the best adventure experiences possible. I worked hard to make better itineraries, to provide better customer service, and to develop better trips than most trekking and guiding companies were offering. As the company has grown, we have not lost sight of this goal.

I believe that you can never sit still in business or in life. You can take satisfaction in your past achievements, but you have to strive to do better if you want to stay the best. Your competitors are always moving forward, and if you aren't also, you are losing ground.

At World Wide Trekking, we want to be the best. We are always updating our gear and services. We try to hire and retain the best possible staff and guides—people who share my passion for the job. We are always trying to offer more trips, better trips—the best adventuring experiences possible, so we have added new locations and experiences. In addition to our many trips to Kilimanjaro and Nepal, we have added trips to Peru, Russia, Ecuador, and Argentina, and we are expanding all the time. We are always looking to come up with the next great adventure for our guests.

After these trips, guests are often not ready to go home, so we have started bundling our treks as part of adventure packages. We couple mountain treks with safaris, sailing, sports adventures, and other activities, working hard to bring the same sense of perfection and uniqueness to these experiences, too.

> What sets World Wide Trekking apart is our passion, our unique adventure packages, and our attention to the little details.

What sets World Wide Trekking apart is our passion, our unique adventure packages, and our attention to the little details. Other agencies do many of the same destinations we do, but they don't offer the extra adventures as part of the package. They don't pay attention to the small details that we do. They rarely include commercial flights, for example, and they don't always help guests with their papers and individual medical needs. We take care of all these details, which results in a more enjoyable and educational experience, and in the end we succeed together in achieving our goals.

At World Wide Trekking, we believe the little details matter. The way you treat people matters. The way we customize our itineraries matters. All of it adds up to a unique and unforgettable experience for our guests. I know this because they tell me so. They tell me how much they appreciate the little things and also the quality, courtesy, and professionalism of our staff.

None of this is to malign any of the hardworking guides who work independently or at other agencies. I only mean to point out that, at World Wide Trekking, we include fees as part of the upfront cost. We don't nickel and dime guests for any of the extras on our trips—it is all included in the package. We also try to customize that package to fit a particular group. If a certain group needs an extra day for a climb, we schedule an extra day.

The goal is to create an environment in which, once guests sign up and show up, the only thing they have to focus on is enjoying themselves the whole time. We want to make it as easy as possible for you to push yourself outside your comfort zone, and we want to be by your side from start to finish, every step of the way.

You may be asking yourself: You want to make it *easy* for me to push myself to my limit and beyond? The answer is a resounding yes! This is not the oxymoron that it sounds like. There is nothing "easy" about trekking to the top of Kilimanjaro, but by removing all the trivial barriers and worries, we free our guests to focus solely on enjoying the experience. They are free to immerse themselves fully in the adventure of the trek without worrying about their papers, making reservations, preparing food, or whether there's an inflated upcharge for those bottles of soda. They are free to focus on getting beyond their comfort zone.

When you come on a trip with World Wide Trekking, my goal is to exceed your expectations on every single aspect of the trip. I want to hear you say, "I can't believe I just did that," or "That's the hardest thing I have ever done," or "That was intense, but it was the best trip I've ever been on." When I hear that you have pushed yourself to the limit and expanded your comfort zone, then and only then do I know that we have succeeded as a company.

Chapter Ten

The Human Outreach Project:
Giving Back

"I expect to pass through this world but once.
Any good, therefore, that I can do or any kindness
I can show to any fellow human being, let me do it now.
Let me not defer or neglect it,
for I shall not pass this way again."
—Stephen Grellet

On the first World Wide Trekking (WWTrek) trip to Mt. Everest Base Camp, in our first year of operating, I planned to take time to visit a nearby orphanage. The year before, one of the Sherpas with whom I worked had been killed in an avalanche in Nepal. We had summited Everest together. He was a very good friend. His three children were now living in an orphanage in Kathmandu. I had raised a few hundred dollars in charitable donations with which I planned to buy them some basic necessities, such as socks, shoes, underwear, coats, and other things. We made a day of it. I took them out to lunch and then shopping. Though I knew Pasang well, I had never met his children, so it was a great honor to get to do this for them.

At the end of the day, I dropped them back off at the orphanage. There were around a hundred other children living there. They eyed the things we had bought for Pasang's children longingly and asked where we had been all day and what we had done. Moments before I had been on cloud nine. Now, I felt horrible. We had swooped in and done this nice thing for three kids, and here were a hundred other orphans, just as deserving, who had gotten nothing.

At that moment, I made a pact with myself: I would do everything I could to give back to the often-underserved communities that World Wide Trekking operates in. I owed my happiness and livelihood to these places. It was the least I could do—the only right thing to do.

This was the genesis of the Human Outreach Project (HOP), a nonprofit organization that I founded to help give back to the communities where World Wide Trekking operates. While I run both World Wide Trekking and Human Outreach Project out of the same office, the two organizations are separate, one being a for-profit enterprise and the other a 501(c)3 nonprofit. However, the two organizations dovetail nicely. Over the years, as I traveled, climbed, and guided, I would always give out little things to people I met along the way—hats, jackets, gear, simple things, whatever I could spare. With HOP, I would expand upon this tradition.

This was a lofty goal, given my circumstances. World Wide Trekking was still in its early days, and struggling to stay afloat. Nonetheless, I was determined to forge ahead with both enterprises. Founding a nonprofit was one of the main reasons I wanted to start my own business in the first place. I believed that more outfitters should have a local social mission to give back to the areas they visit. Rather than wait for that to happen, I decided, as Gandhi said, to "Be the change I wanted to see in the world." So I started and ran both operations together. I had made a commitment to the orphanage in Kathmandu—and to our humanitarian efforts elsewhere—that I didn't want to back out on. It seemed only natural for World Wide Trekking and the Human Outreach Project to rise up together.

As with most great undertakings, we started small. We collected donated money and supplies for HOP to bring with us on World Wide Trekking trips. We packed hygiene kits and medical supplies and other necessities into duffel bags and checked them at the airline gate. I started with one bag, then two, then more. Eventually, this would become too much to handle, and we started raising money to buy supplies in the places we visited. But when we were starting out, we took donations of actual physical goods and packed them on the plane. We would take anything we could get that would be of use.

We tried to do things that would help whole communities rather than just a single person, which is why we focused on providing supplies to medical clinics and orphanages. However, I wasn't happy to just give money and supplies. If HOP was going to have a lasting impact, it would need to undertake self-sustaining projects that would help build stronger communities. We wanted to build infrastructure and start sustained community programs. We wanted to

> We wanted to make an ongoing difference, not just give handouts and walk away. It is better to provide people with things that would last, such as buildings and farm animals, rather than just money. We work hard to empower the local communities by empowering the local people.

make an ongoing difference, not just give handouts and walk away. It is better to provide people with things that would last, such as buildings and farm animals, rather than just money. We work hard to empower the local communities by empowering the local people.

One of our first big projects was supporting an orphanage in Tanzania. We had been supporting a medical clinic and orphanage there by giving them supplies, but we wanted to do more. My goal was to engage in large projects that would be sustainable. For example, the children at the orphanage needed more food. Rather than just give them food, we decided to get them milk cows. I built a corral with the help of a few college students. We dug holes, sunk beams, and poured concrete. Two weeks later, we had a corral and milk cows that were delivering twenty liters of milk per day to the orphanage.

Our biggest obstacle was corruption, which was another reason I was uncomfortable just supplying money and goods. Things went missing all the time. At the orphanage, it started with the hygiene kits we brought over for the kids. We would drop them off and then come back two weeks later to find them gone, even though they should have lasted months, or even years. No one uses hygiene kits that quickly. On one occasion we purchased a set of mosquito nets for the entire orphanage to protect the kids from malaria. We dropped them off on our way to Kilimanjaro, and they were gone by the time we came back off the mountain. They should have lasted for years.

The mosquito nets were the last straw. This was something no one could deny—they should have lasted years. Mosquito nets don't just disappear unless someone takes them. That meant one thing: they had been taken and sold. I simply couldn't abide this. They had been purchased with donated money. I couldn't conscionably continue to take money for things that were going to be sold on the black market. We stopped all donations to the medical clinic and the orphanage that we had been supporting in Tanzania.

However, I was not about to let this deter me from our mission. I recognized then that the only way we could control corruption in a remote area was to build our own orphanage, staff it with our own people, and run it from the ground up. We began to look for land where we could do just that. That winter, we bought a four-acre tract of land in Tanzania and started applying for a "constitution," which is basically a government permit that allows you to run an orphanage legally. We assembled a board, on which I am the only non-Tanzanian person—the rest are all locals.

In the spring of 2009, I stepped onto the land for the first time. It was just this dusty, empty field in the middle of nowhere. There was no running water, no electricity, no buildings, no nothing. Just a barren field with Kilimanjaro looming in the background. For a moment, I felt in over my head, a feeling I would have many times over the next three years of construction. But as with any other big project, be it summiting a mountain or starting a business, I knew what I had to do: banish negative thinking, consider the big picture, roll up my sleeves, and focus on the task in front of me.

We had a lot going for us already. The site was great. It was in a good location, with great views of Kilimanjaro. It was only fifteen minutes from the international airport. We had good access to the main road, but it was just far enough off the road to be nice and quiet. This was, I realized, a great place for an orphanage, and I knew we were on the right track.

We drafted up a plan to build the orphanage in phases. This allowed us to focus on an achievable short-term goal (an open-air building that wouldn't require plumbing or electricity) without losing sight of the big picture. The first year, we fenced in the four acres, planted 185 trees, and built a pavilion that would serve as a commons area and meeting place. It was the easiest building to start, and I wanted to break ground in order to get some momentum building so we would have something to show potential donors when fundraising.

By the end of the summer we had the pavilion built, but we were still a long way from opening our doors. Over the course of the next two years, we built a dormitory. Everything went slowly and laboriously. No electricity meant no power tools. We mixed cement on the ground and put it in five-gallon buckets because we had no wheelbarrow or cement mixer. We carried in water with donkeys. We hired local craftsmen to help the students and me build bunk beds, tables, chairs, counters, and everything else. I helped with much of this work myself. When we had big projects, I would check in on the local craftsmen between World Wide Trekking trips.

At this point, we ran into financial troubles. While we were collecting donations from clients and contacts made through World Wide Trekking, I had moral qualms with doing heavy fundraising before we actually had children living there. What if we folded, and all of the money we raised had been wasted? That was hard for me to deal with, so we held few big fundraisers. I was grateful to a few dedicated HOP donors, but eventually the money ran out. To make it through those early years, I had to divert money from World Wide Trekking into the Human Outreach Project. This was a dicey proposition. World Wide Trekking was new and squeaking by on razor-thin margins. Still, I was committed. Over the next few years, I spent tens of thousands of dollars of WWTrek money on finishing the orphanage.

By the end of the third year, we had built the pavilion, a dormitory, public restrooms, and the first phase of the kitchen. We split the dorm in half so that we could have a girls' side and a boys' side. The staff had separate quarters as well. The facility was basic and incomplete, but now functioning. We were able to get water onsite before the opening, but we had no electric lines. We used solar power for lighting and wood burning for cooking. We planted gardens and corn in the fields.

The HOP Kilimanjaro Kids Community was ready to go. The Tanzanian government finally approved our permits, and we were now ready to bring in our first kids. Though we had beds for more, we started with only ten children; I couldn't bear the thought of running out of money once they were in our care. So we started slowly. Never in my life have I taken on such a great responsibility. I was suddenly responsible for all of these kids' welfare and future. When problems arose, the buck stopped with me. I took that very seriously, and was careful not to get in too far over my head. Taking on too many new kids would jeopardize the ones already there. We started with only ten, and even now, at the writing of this book, we have only thirteen kids—but they are thirteen awesome, amazing kids whose lives have been forever changed!

There were times, especially early on, when I questioned what we were doing. I remember one time in particular when I went with Raymond, my operations manager at the orphanage, to pick up two children from a mother who could not care for them. She was sick and dying, and the children's father had already died. We arrived at an abandoned shack where they were squatting. The mother was lying on a blanket on the floor with two children—a girl, Nema, and a boy, Nehemiah. They were about two and seven years old, respectively. They sat next to their mother on the dirt floor.

Raymond went over the paperwork with the mother in Swahili. She then signed over the kids to the orphanage. I had expected an emotional situation in the shack, but the mother was smiling. At first, I was confused, but then it became clear that she was relieved that the children would have a safe place to go and be cared for.

The family said their goodbyes, and we took the children out to the car. I sat Nema in my lap. Raymond started the car. As we started to back out, the children suddenly understood that we were taking them away from their mother. As we started to pull away, Nema let out a long, shrill shriek. At that moment I really questioned what we were doing. Was it right? Why did I have the right to do this? What was really best for the kids? Who was I to think I knew what was best? What if I failed? I tried my best to banish this negative thinking, but it was difficult. The situation felt confusing … and suddenly very, very real.

When we got back to the orphanage, we introduced the two children to their caretakers and fed them stew and water. They lapped at it furiously. They were so hungry—literally starving. The caretakers got them cleaned up and into new clothes. Nema had a scowl on her face the whole time. For days, she moped around with a pouty lip.

I had to leave them to take a group up Kilimanjaro. By the time I got back, Nema was starting to adjust to her new life. I'm sure she still missed her mother, but she now had a home and a bed, and people to feed and care for her. I could see that she was starting to enjoy her new life, and the scowl was disappearing.

Nema is still at the orphanage. She is five years old now. She is in school, learning English, and she has the biggest smile you have ever seen. Seeing her and the other children adjust so well and thrive has made the whole process worthwhile. When we first took her from her mother, I had had my doubts, but no longer. We were doing the right thing with Nema—with all of the children. We were making a positive difference in these children's lives. I could see it in Nema as clearly as with any of our children.

Our joy in the positive effect we have on these few children is tempered by the fact that there are so many more we cannot help. Engaging in any kind of humanitarian effort requires one to accept a certain dose of realism. There are millions of children who could use the same help. Even just in Tanzania, there are tens of thousands of children we would take in if only we could. But we can't. We don't have the space or the resources. Knowing this stirs up the same feelings I had at the orphanage in Kathmandu, when I felt guilty for helping Pasang's children but none of the others at the orphanage.

The difference is that this time, there really is nothing I can do. We cannot save everyone. We are doing the best we can do with the ones we have. Rather than bringing in as many kids as we can manage to feed, my idea has always been to keep the orphanage small enough that we can give not just food and a roof to our kids, but better futures. We want not just to care for them, but to offer them the best quality of life we can while preparing them for the future by educating them and teaching them to be good people.

That said, we do our best to have the greatest and widest effect that we can while staying true to our mission. We do our best to try to help the whole community, not just the kids in our beds. There is a ripple effect of the work we do: We hire local staff and contractors. We have hired groundskeepers, guards, construction workers, caretakers, cooks, cleaners, and more. In an economically depressed region, jobs like these can change lives. The orphanage benefits the entire community economically, not just the children.

My goal with HOP is to create an impact that is far-reaching and sustained. Partly this means involving a large swath of the community in our activities, be it through direct services, employment, or in any other manner. It also means creating change that lasts. My goal for the orphanage is to create an institution that is as self-sustainable as possible. We have a vegetable garden, four milk cows, a dozen hens for eggs, and even more goats. We raise chickens for meat for the staff and children, as well as for sale. All these endeavors make the orphanage more self-reliant while also teaching the kids real life skills that they can use throughout their lives.

We try to stay forward-thinking. It is great to be able to give the children a home, but there is no way we can care for them forever. We start by giving them a safe place, a roof over their heads, and food to eat. When they first come to us, that's what they need. But that isn't enough though to set them up for success. Eventually, they will grow up and leave the orphanage, and when they do, we want them ready to succeed in life.

The number one thing that will make a difference is education. The best paying jobs in Tanzania are in the tourism industry. There are good jobs working on the safaris and in the lodges, but candidates must be able to speak English. Education is the key to our kids' futures. Right now, they are young—all of our children are between three and twelve years old at the writing of this book—but eventually they will grow up and have to compete in the workforce. In the long run, the most important thing we can do is not to give them things, but to help them become independent and self-sufficient. This is why we had a tutor come in to teach them. We now have all thirteen of our children enrolled in formal school so they can learn English and get a proper education. Our schoolroom is now the HOP Kilimanjaro Kids Community Learning Center, where they can go to study and use the Internet.

Another way we seek to have a wider impact is by encouraging people to get involved. We collect donations through the Human

Outreach Project and use World Wide Trekking as a way to get the word out about our humanitarian efforts. Not only do we solicit donations, we try to get guests directly involved in HOP. On most WWTrek trips, we dedicate a part of one day to introduce guests to the needs and struggles of local communities and to engage guests in humanitarian efforts. We might visit medical clinics in impoverished areas and donate medical supplies, or visit an orphanage to donate clothes and hygiene kits. We try to custom-tailor humanitarianism so that it benefits the target community and doesn't inadvertently cause problems for anyone.

On WWTrek trips to Kilimanjaro, we usually do a site tour of the HOP Kilimanjaro Kids Community. Depending on the trekking group, we sometimes spend time with the kids, playing a game of soccer, reading a book aloud, or some other activity. Our guests often find the experience eye opening. By booking their trips with us, and also by donating and volunteering, they get to do their small part to give back to the communities in the areas where they travel. That's what HOP is all about.

We also offer what we call voluntourism opportunities for students and community members to help with HOP projects. Typically, volunteers will come for a week or so and help with a specific project. While many of our projects are long term, like the orphanage, we try to give volunteers specific projects that they can see through to the finish, such as building bunk beds at the orphanage.

Other projects are reactions to short-term crises. For example, when an avalanche killed a dozen Sherpas in the 2014 season—the deadliest single day ever on Mt. Everest—we held a fundraiser at Snowbird and raised $27,000 for the Sherpas and their families.

In addition to our efforts abroad, we also give back to the local community where our offices are in Salt Lake City. We just sponsored a Thanksgiving dinner for local veterans dealing with PTSD (Post Traumatic Stress Disorder), providing a full-course meal for the veterans and their families that they could prepare in their own homes. We then did the same thing for Christmas, and this time we bought gifts for their children—all thirty-six of them! I realize this is a small thing, but it is also a good thing, and we hope to grow the program this year and do more in our local community as well.

As you can see, we have our hands in a lot of different things. I am always looking for ways to further expand what we do, but we are careful to move slowly and deliberately whenever we enter a new place. You have to be culturally sensitive and attuned to what communities need. It doesn't do any good to go in and hand out things that will just be stolen and sold, or that are of little use. We start by building relationships within the communities we visit and learning what the community needs so that we can focus our efforts to help in the most beneficial way we can.

As with World Wide Trekking, our greatest asset at HOP is our people. We have a board of trustees that functions as an advisory board, and to which I report to a couple of times per year. I cannot thank them enough, especially our chair, Sue Goldie, who is also a professor and director of Harvard's School of Public Health and founding faculty director of Harvard's Global Health Institute. I am lucky to have this well-respected group behind me and HOP. I value them just as I value the local staff at the HOP Kilimanjaro Kids Community, and all the other people who have helped to make HOP a success.

HOP has put me outside my comfort zone again and again. I have always been aware of the risks of spending other people's donated money, but now, as we grow our efforts, the responsibility of caring for multiple children whose unknown future I will be a part of is heavy at times.

My hope is that, just as the rest of this book is meant to push you outside your comfort zone to engage in adventures you never thought possible, this chapter will push you to open up your heart and engage the world in new ways that help your fellow man. If this book has pushed you to want to join us on one of our World Wide Trekking trips, I hope you will also want to give back to the communities that make these places so special. I believe that most people are good people, and want to help others, but we don't always know how. But all you really have to do is get out there and start looking, make connections with others in the community, and give just a little of yourself.

Afterword

by Dean Cardinale

Thank you for taking the time to read this book. Storytelling is an important part of being a guide. Stories are one way—perhaps the oldest way—that people teach one another and share wisdom. My great hope here is that you turn this page, set the book down, and walk away enriched by experiences and perspectives that may be different from your own.

If you take one thing away from this book, let it be this: always expect more from life and from yourself. At the beginning of this book, I shared my experiences living in a tent in the woods as a shiftless young ski bum. This is something I rarely talk about, and I only share it here because it was a turning point in my new life out west. My life got better when I told myself I wasn't going to accept my circumstances.

Don't ever settle for the "tent in the woods," unless, of course, that is what you want most from life. Don't just make something of yourself—make yourself into exactly who and what you want to be.

In my experience, figuring out what you want to do with your life means making a choice to push yourself outside your comfort zone. Embrace exploration, and then, when you find the path that's right for you, put in the work to make the journey a successful one.

Don't ever be satisfied with past victories. Keep searching and keep exploring. Always set higher standards and loftier goals for yourself. Dream big—and then go out and chase those dreams.

Don't underestimate yourself. You can accomplish great things in life if you have vision and are willing to work hard. You will face setbacks on the way; everyone does. Just remember—setbacks aren't failures. The stories in this book are full of setbacks. Often I had to abandon goals and adopt new plans when things weren't going the way I had anticipated or hoped for. I have had to turn back and climb down mountains without summiting. I have had to abandon business strategies and enterprises that weren't working. I have had to start over many times.

Rather than view these experiences as failures, I choose to see them as opportunities to grow and learn. When I try again, I do so with the invaluable and heard-earned wisdom one only gains from experience—from going out and doing the thing, suffering so-called failure, and then trying again.

You just have to keep plugging away, keep trying, and put one foot in front of the other. Keep on keeping on at a slow and methodical pace, and you will go far in time. Recognize and learn from setbacks, change your plans if you have to, but don't stop moving forward. Keep trying harder. When the mountain—or life—pushes you, always push back.

I leave you with one final favorite quotation of mine.

> *"The greatest danger for most of us lies not*
> *in setting our aim too high and falling short,*
> *but in setting our aim too low and achieving our mark."*
> —Michelangelo